MW01690702

LENTEN *GOSPEL* REFLECTIONS

BISHOP ROBERT BARRON

WORD on FIRE

Published by Word on Fire, Elk Grove Village, IL 60007
© 2026 by Word on Fire Catholic Ministries
Printed in the United States of America
All rights reserved

Cover design by Megan Travers, typesetting by Marlene Burrell, and interior art direction by Cassie Bielak and Katherine Spitler

Excerpts from the *Lectionary for Mass for Use in the Dioceses of the United States of America, second typical edition* © 2001, 1998, 1997, 1986, 1970 Confraternity of Christian Doctrine, Inc., Washington, DC. Used with permission. All rights reserved. No portion of this text may be reproduced by any means without permission in writing from the copyright owner.

No other part of this book may be used or reproduced in any manner whatsoever without written permission, except in the case of brief quotations in critical articles or reviews. For more information, contact Word on Fire Catholic Ministries, PO Box 97330, Washington, DC 20090-7330 or email contact@wordonfire.org.

ISBN: 978-1-68578-290-0

Library of Congress Control Number: 2025943360

INTRODUCTION

Friends,

Thank you for joining me as we journey together toward the great feast of Easter!

Lent is a season for refocusing on the suffering and death of our Lord Jesus Christ, so that we will be ready to embrace the good news of the Resurrection.

Why this emphasis on suffering? Because Christ saved us through an act of suffering. He bore in his own person the weight of our sin and died for us on the cross, where suffering and love coincided.

And the Church is the Body of Christ, which participates in Christ. Therefore, we shouldn't be surprised that we will be called upon to suffer out of love. In the economy of grace, God may use our suffering to bear the burden of another member of the Body of Christ, just as one system can take up the work of another, or one organ can support another.

So as we begin with Ash Wednesday, let us resolve to focus on Christ's suffering, and to unite our own suffering—through fasting, prayer, almsgiving, and reflection on the Stations of the Cross—with the suffering members of the Church. It is not the destination but the journey that will ultimately transform us.

Peace,

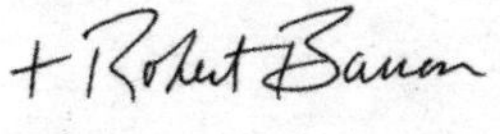

Bishop Robert Barron

LENTEN *GOSPEL* REFLECTIONS

FEBRUARY 18, 2026

Ash Wednesday

Matthew 6:1–6, 16–18

Jesus said to his disciples: "Take care not to perform righteous deeds in order that people may see them; otherwise, you will have no recompense from your heavenly Father. When you give alms, do not blow a trumpet before you, as the hypocrites do in the synagogues and in the streets to win the praise of others. Amen, I say to you, they have received their reward. But when you give alms, do not let your left hand know what your right is doing, so that your almsgiving may be secret. And your Father who sees in secret will repay you.

"When you pray, do not be like the hypocrites, who love to stand and pray in the synagogues and on street corners so that others may see them. Amen, I say to you, they have received their reward. But when you pray, go to your inner room, close the door, and pray to your Father in secret. And your Father who sees in secret will repay you.

"When you fast, do not look gloomy like the hypocrites. They neglect their appearance, so that they may appear to others to be fasting. Amen, I say to you, they have received their reward. But when you fast, anoint your head and wash your face, so that you may not appear to be fasting, except to your Father who is hidden. And your Father who sees what is hidden will repay you."

Friends, in today's Gospel, Jesus prescribes the essential disciplines of prayer, fasting, and almsgiving. Let's focus on fasting and almsgiving.

The appetites for food and drink are so pressing, so elemental, that, unless they are quelled and disciplined, they will simply take over the soul. They are like children who clamor constantly for attention and who, if indulged, will in short order run the house.

Therefore, if the passion for God is to be awakened, the more immediately pressing desires must be muted, and this is the purpose of fasting. We go hungry and thirsty so that the deepest hunger and thirst might be felt. In a way, fasting is like the "calming of the monkey mind" effected by the Rosary: both are means of settling the superficial mind that darts from preoccupation to preoccupation.

But food and drink are not the only objects of concupiscent desire. Material things and wealth are also ready substitutes for the passion for God. Thus, a kind of fasting from what money can buy is an important practice. How often Jesus recommends that his disciples give to the poor, and how often throughout the Christian tradition has almsgiving been emphasized.

Reflect: This Lenten season, what are some ways you can find your security not in food, drink, money, or material things but in Jesus Christ?

FEBRUARY 19, 2026

Thursday after Ash Wednesday

Luke 9:22–25

Jesus said to his disciples: "The Son of Man must suffer greatly and be rejected by the elders, the chief priests, and the scribes, and be killed and on the third day be raised."

Then he said to all, "If anyone wishes to come after me, he must deny himself and take up his cross daily and follow me. For whoever wishes to save his life will lose it, but whoever loses his life for my sake will save it. What profit is there for one to gain the whole world yet lose or forfeit himself?"

Friends, our Gospel today lays out Jesus' conditions for discipleship. For all of us sinners, to varying degrees, our own lives have become god. That is to say, we see the universe turning around our ego, our needs, our projects, our plans, and our likes and dislikes. True conversion—the *metanoia* that Jesus talks about—is so much more than moral reform, though it includes that. It has to do with a complete shift in consciousness, a whole new way of looking at one's life.

Jesus offered a teaching that must have been gut-wrenching to his first-century audience: "If anyone wishes to come after me, he must deny himself and take up his cross daily and follow me." His listeners knew what the cross meant: a death in utter agony, nakedness, and humiliation. They didn't think of the cross automatically in religious terms, as we do. They knew it in all of its awful power.

Unless you crucify your ego, you cannot be my follower, Jesus says. This move—this terrible move—has to be the foundation of the spiritual life.

Reflect: How do you think about suffering in your life? Do you read it simply as meaningless pain or as a participation in the cross?

FEBRUARY 20, 2026

Friday after Ash Wednesday

Matthew 9:14–15

The disciples of John approached Jesus and said, "Why do we and the Pharisees fast much, but your disciples do not fast?" Jesus answered them, "Can the wedding guests mourn as long as the bridegroom is with them? The days will come when the bridegroom is taken away from them, and then they will fast."

Friends, in today's Gospel, people ask Jesus why he and his disciples do not fast when John and his disciples do. Jesus' answer is wonderful: "Can the wedding guests mourn as long as the bridegroom is with them?" (That's a typically Jewish style, by the way—answering a question with another question.)

This great image of the wedding feast comes up frequently in the New Testament, most obviously in the narrative of the wedding feast at Cana.

And it is echoed in the tradition. Jesus is the wedding of heaven and earth, the marriage of divinity and humanity; he is the Bridegroom and the Church is the Bride. In him, the most intimate union is achieved between God and the world.

Could you imagine people fasting at a wedding banquet? Could you imagine going into an elegant room with your fellow guests and being served bread and water? It would be ridiculous! So, says Jesus: "The days will come when the bridegroom is taken away from them, and then they will fast." The mark of the Christian dispensation is joy, exuberance, and delight. God and the world have come together. What could be better news?

Reflect: Do you sometimes feel that Christianity is almost too good to be true? How can you better take in and share the Good News, even amid the suffering and darkness of the world?

FEBRUARY 21, 2026

Saturday after Ash Wednesday

Luke 5:27–32

Jesus saw a tax collector named Levi sitting at the customs post. He said to him, "Follow me." And leaving everything behind, he got up and followed him. Then Levi gave a great banquet for him in his house, and a large crowd of tax collectors and others were at table with them. The Pharisees and their scribes complained to his disciples, saying, "Why do you eat and drink with tax collectors and sinners?" Jesus said to them in reply, "Those who are healthy do not need a physician, but the sick do. I have not come to call the righteous to repentance but sinners."

Friends, in today's Gospel, Jesus tells Matthew, "Follow me." The call of Jesus addresses the mind, but it is meant to move through the mind into the body, and through the body into the whole of one's life, into the most practical of moves and decisions. "Follow me" has the sense of "apprentice to me" or "walk as I walk; think as I think; choose as I choose." Discipleship entails an entire reworking of the self according to the pattern and manner of Jesus.

Upon hearing the address of the Lord, the tax collector, we are told, "got up and followed him." The Greek word behind "got up" is *anastas*, the same word used to describe the Resurrection (*anastasis*) of Jesus from the dead. Following Jesus is indeed a kind of resurrection from the dead, since it involves the transition from a lower form of life to a higher, from a preoccupation with the temporary goods of this world to an immersion in the goodness of God.

Those who have undergone a profound conversion tend to speak of their former life as a kind of illusion, something not entirely real. Thus Paul can say, "I live, no longer I, but Christ lives in me"; Thomas Merton can speak of the "false self" that has given way to the authentic self; and, perhaps most movingly, the father of the prodigal son can say, "Your brother was dead and has come to life again; he was lost and has been found."

Reflect: In what dimensions of the Church's life—the liturgy, the Eucharist, the proclamation of the Scriptures, the summons to moral excellence, the lives of the saints—have you experienced the call of Jesus to conversion?

FEBRUARY 22, 2026

First Sunday of Lent

Matthew 4:1–11

At that time Jesus was led by the Spirit into the desert to be tempted by the devil. He fasted for forty days and forty nights, and afterwards he was hungry. The tempter approached and said to him, "If you are the Son of God, command that these stones become loaves of bread. He said in reply, "It is written:

One does not live on bread alone,
but on every word that comes forth
from the mouth of God."

Then the devil took him to the holy city, and made him stand on the parapet of the temple, and said to him, "If you are the Son of God, throw yourself down. For it is written:

He will command his angels concerning you
and with their hands they will support you,
lest you dash your foot against a stone."

Jesus answered him, "Again it is written, *You shall not put the Lord, your God, to the test.*" Then the devil took him up to a very high mountain, and showed him all the kingdoms of the world in their magnificence, and he said to him, "All these I shall give to you, if you will prostrate yourself and worship me." At this, Jesus said to him, "Get away, Satan! It is written:

The Lord, your God, shall you worship
and him alone shall you serve."

Then the devil left him and, behold, angels came and ministered to him.

Friends, today's Gospel tells of the Lord's temptation in the desert. After forty days of fasting in the desert (evocative of Israel's forty years of wandering in the desert), Jesus meets the devil, who proceeds to lure the Messiah onto the path of sin. Jesus' sacrifice will entail his coming to battle sin at close quarters, his willingness, therefore, to be drawn by its power, to come under its sway.

Satan first tempts him with sensual pleasure: "If you are the Son of God, command that these stones become loaves of bread." One of the most elemental forms of spiritual dysfunction is to make the satisfaction of sensual desire the center of one's life. Jesus responds: "One does not live on bread alone, but on every word that comes forth from the mouth of God."

Jesus enters, through psychological and spiritual identification, into the condition of the person lured by this sin, but then he manages to withstand the temptation and in fact to twist this perversion back to rectitude.

Reflect: How are you moved away from the will and purposes of God through the satisfaction of the most immediate needs of the body? In what ways can you resist these immediate and insistent desires that so easily dominate the soul?

FEBRUARY 23, 2026

Monday of the First Week of Lent

Matthew 25:31–46

Jesus said to his disciples: "When the Son of Man comes in his glory, and all the angels with him, he will sit upon his glorious throne, and all the nations will be assembled before him. And he will separate them one from another, as a shepherd separates the sheep from the goats. He will place the sheep on his right and the goats on his left. Then the king will say to those on his right, 'Come, you who are blessed by my Father. Inherit the kingdom prepared for you from the foundation of the world. For I was hungry and you gave me food, I was thirsty and you gave me drink, a stranger and you welcomed me, naked and you clothed me, ill and you cared for me, in prison and you visited me.' Then the righteous will answer him and say, 'Lord, when did we see you hungry and feed you, or thirsty and give you drink? When did we see you a stranger and welcome you, or naked and clothe you? When did we see you ill or in prison, and visit you?' And the king will say to them in reply, 'Amen, I say to you, whatever you did for one of these least brothers of mine, you did for me.' Then he will say to those on his left, 'Depart from me, you accursed, into the eternal fire prepared for the Devil and his angels. For I was hungry and you gave me no food, I was thirsty and you gave me no drink, a stranger and you gave me no welcome, naked and you gave me no clothing, ill and in prison, and you did not care for me.' Then they will answer and say, 'Lord, when did we see you hungry or thirsty or a stranger or naked or ill or in prison, and not minister to your needs?' He will answer them, 'Amen, I say to you, what you did not do for one of these least ones, you did not do for me.' And these will go off to eternal punishment, but the righteous to eternal life."

Friends, our Gospel today is the scene of the Last Judgment. We hear that the specifics are a matter of love concretely expressed: "For I was hungry and you gave me food, I was thirsty and you gave me drink, a stranger and you welcomed me, naked and you clothed me, ill and you cared for me, in prison and you visited me." And we know the famous connection that Jesus makes: "Whatever you did for one of these least brothers of mine, you did for me."

There is something awful about the specificity of these demands. This is not love in the abstract, having affection for "humanity."

It is caring for *that person* who is homeless, for *that person* who is ill, for *that person* who is in prison.

We do not take our money, our social status, our worldly power into the next world; but we do take the quality of our love. You might consider doing an examination of conscience at the end of each day, and use as your criterion this passage. Perhaps put it up on your wall or post it next to your bed so that you see it before you go to sleep.

Reflect: Dorothy Day once said that everything a baptized person does, every day, should be directly or indirectly related to the corporal and spiritual works of mercy. What are you doing to incorporate these works in your own life?

FEBRUARY 24, 2026

Tuesday of the First Week of Lent

Matthew 6:7–15

Jesus said to his disciples: "In praying, do not babble like the pagans, who think that they will be heard because of their many words. Do not be like them. Your Father knows what you need before you ask him.

"This is how you are to pray:

Our Father who art in heaven,
    hallowed be thy name,
    thy Kingdom come,
thy will be done,
    on earth as it is in heaven.
Give us this day our daily bread;
and forgive us our trespasses,
    as we forgive those who trespass against us;
and lead us not into temptation,
    but deliver us from evil.

"If you forgive men their transgressions, your heavenly Father will forgive you. But if you do not forgive men, neither will your Father forgive your transgressions."

Friends, the Gospel for today is a great moment, for in it the Son of God teaches us to pray. Our teacher is not just a guru, a spiritual sage, or a religious genius, but the Son of God. This is why the Our Father is the model of all prayer.

A desire to pray is planted deep within us, the desire to speak to God and to listen to him. We can forget to pray, neglect to pray, become lazy in prayer, but we can never really lose the desire to pray.

And so let us attend carefully to the first words of Jesus' great prayer: "Our Father who art in heaven, hallowed be thy name." Our basic problem is getting our priorities mixed up. We seek all kinds of worldly things—money, pleasure, power, honor—all of which are unsatisfying.

What we should desire, first, is God. This is precisely what the prayer to hallow the name of God is all about. It's not that God's name isn't in fact hallowed, but we're praying that we might keep it that way, that we might honor God in all things. We're praying for a radical reorientation of our consciousness.

Reflect: Meditate on how everything in your spiritual life flows from this prioritization: "Hear, O Israel: The Lord is our God, the Lord alone" (Deut. 6:4); "Love the Lord your God with all your heart, and with all your soul, and with all your mind" (Matt. 22:37).

FEBRUARY 25, 2026

Wednesday of the First Week of Lent

Luke 11:29–32

While still more people gathered in the crowd, Jesus said to them, "This generation is an evil generation; it seeks a sign, but no sign will be given it, except the sign of Jonah. Just as Jonah became a sign to the Ninevites, so will the Son of Man be to this generation. At the judgment the queen of the south will rise with the men of this generation and she will condemn them, because she came from the ends of the earth to hear the wisdom of Solomon, and there is something greater than Solomon here. At the judgment the men of Nineveh will arise with this generation and condemn it, because at the preaching of Jonah they repented, and there is something greater than Jonah here."

Friends, in today's Gospel, Jesus tells the crowds who seek a sign that they will only receive the sign of Jonah: "Just as Jonah became a sign to the Ninevites, so will the Son of Man be to this generation."

Jonah is called by God to preach to Nineveh, which is described as an enormously large city. It takes, they say, three days to walk through it. I can't help but think of Nineveh as one of our large, modern cities, a center of all sorts of worldly activity and preoccupation.

What would its conversion look like? A turning back to God as the only enduring good. After hearing the word of Jonah, the Ninevites proclaim a fast, and all of them, great and small, put on sackcloth. What is the purpose of these ascetic practices? To wean people away from an attachment to worldly pleasures.

Go beyond the mind that you have. Repent. Live as though nothing in this world finally matters. And you will be living in the kingdom of God!

Reflect: Has there been a particular worldly good that you were once attached to, one that tied you down in the spiritual life? How were you freed to follow the promptings of the Lord?

FEBRUARY 26, 2026

Thursday of the First Week of Lent

Matthew 7:7–12

Jesus said to his disciples: "Ask and it will be given to you; seek and you will find; knock and the door will be opened to you. For everyone who asks, receives; and the one who seeks, finds; and to the one who knocks, the door will be opened. Which one of you would hand his son a stone when he asked for a loaf of bread, or a snake when he asked for a fish? If you then, who are wicked, know how to give good gifts to your children, how much more will your heavenly Father give good things to those who ask him.

"Do to others whatever you would have them do to you. This is the law and the prophets."

Friends, today's Gospel urges us to persist in prayer. The Lord wants us to ask with persistence, even stubbornness.

Now, we must not think of God as becoming exasperated by our prayer of petition, but the clear implication is that we *will* get what we want through persistence: "Ask and it will be given to you; seek and you will find; knock and the door will be opened to you."

How do we make sense of this? For me, the best explanation is offered by St. Augustine. He said that God doesn't always immediately give us what we ask for, and in fact, he compels us to ask again and again. The Lord wants to stretch us, expanding our desire so as to receive the gift he desires to give us.

If we got everything we wanted, right away and without effort, we wouldn't appreciate what we've received, and we wouldn't really be capable of taking it in. It would be like pouring new wine into old, shrunken wineskins, resulting in a loss of both the skins and the wine.

So if the gift doesn't come right away, don't despair; rather, feel your very soul expanding in anticipation.

Reflect: Meditate on a time when you brought a persistent request to God in prayer, and God—like a good parent—did not respond the way you would have liked him to. How did his refusal compel your heart to expand?

FEBRUARY 27, 2026

Friday of the First Week of Lent

Matthew 5:20–26

Jesus said to his disciples: "I tell you, unless your righteousness surpasses that of the scribes and Pharisees, you will not enter into the Kingdom of heaven.

"You have heard that it was said to your ancestors, *You shall not kill; and whoever kills will be liable to judgment.* But I say to you, whoever is angry with his brother will be liable to judgment, and whoever says to his brother, *Raqa,* will be answerable to the Sanhedrin, and whoever says, 'You fool,' will be liable to fiery Gehenna. Therefore, if you bring your gift to the altar, and there recall that your brother has anything against you, leave your gift there at the altar, go first and be reconciled with your brother, and then come and offer your gift. Settle with your opponent quickly while on the way to court. Otherwise your opponent will hand you over to the judge, and the judge will hand you over to the guard, and you will be thrown into prison. Amen, I say to you, you will not be released until you have paid the last penny."

Friends, in today's Gospel, Jesus commands us to be reconciled with one another. I want to say something about the role of forgiveness in repairing our broken relationships.

When you are at worship and realize that you need to forgive someone (or be forgiven by someone), go and do it. Go get reconciled, then come back. It's like a rule of physics. There is something hidden in the deep mystery of God, and I can't fully explicate it. Somehow, if there is a lack of forgiveness in you, it blocks the movement of God in you. Perhaps it's simply because God is love, and so whatever is opposed to love in us blocks the flow of God's power and God's life.

One reason we do not forgive is that we feel that some injustice has been done to us, and we resent it. A good cure for this feeling is to kneel before the cross of Jesus. What do you see there? The innocent Son of God nailed to the cross—the ultimate injustice. What does he do? He forgives his persecutors. Meditate on that, and your sense of being treated unjustly will fade away.

Reflect: Is there a grudge that you're nursing right now—a particular person whom you are struggling with and refusing to forgive? Spend a minute kneeling before a crucifix, then reflect on how you might go and be reconciled with him or her.

FEBRUARY 28, 2026

Saturday of the First Week of Lent

Matthew 5:43–48

Jesus said to his disciples: "You have heard that it was said, *You shall love your neighbor and hate your enemy*. But I say to you, love your enemies, and pray for those who persecute you, that you may be children of your heavenly Father, for he makes his sun rise on the bad and the good, and causes rain to fall on the just and the unjust. For if you love those who love you, what recompense will you have? Do not the tax collectors do the same? And if you greet your brothers and sisters only, what is unusual about that? Do not the pagans do the same? So be perfect, just as your heavenly Father is perfect."

Friends, in today's Gospel, Jesus commands us to love our enemies.

The first reason we love our enemies is because this is the best way to test the quality of our love. Love is not primarily an emotion but an act of the will. It is willing the good of the other as other.

A second reason to love your enemies is that they tell you about yourself. There is a very good chance that the people who most bother you are those who most reveal to you unsavory truths about yourself.

Third, perhaps the person you consider your enemy is actually pointing out to you the inadequacy of your own life. Maybe he is right and good, and it's you who are off-center. Could it be that your enemy is in fact a kind of saint who is indirectly indicating your own weakness and lack of moral courage?

A final reason to love your enemies: you might win them back.

Reflect: Hold an enemy in mind: first, a more general or global enemy, then a more personal enemy. What do these enemies reveal to you about yourself? In what ways can you follow Christ's teaching that you must love precisely these people?

MARCH 1, 2026

Second Sunday of Lent

Matthew 17:1–9

Jesus took Peter, James, and John his brother, and led them up a high mountain by themselves. And he was transfigured before them; his face shone like the sun and his clothes became white as light. And behold, Moses and Elijah appeared to them, conversing with him. Then Peter said to Jesus in reply, "Lord, it is good that we are here. If you wish, I will make three tents here, one for you, one for Moses, and one for Elijah." While he was still speaking, behold, a bright cloud cast a shadow over them, then from the cloud came a voice that said, "This is my beloved Son, with whom I am well pleased; listen to him." When the disciples heard this, they fell prostrate and were very much afraid. But Jesus came and touched them, saying, "Rise, and do not be afraid." And when the disciples raised their eyes, they saw no one else but Jesus alone.

As they were coming down from the mountain, Jesus charged them, "Do not tell the vision to anyone until the Son of Man has been raised from the dead."

Friends, today's Gospel celebrates the Transfiguration.

Christ came not just to make us nice people or morally upright folks, but rather to give us a share in his divine life, to make us denizens of heaven, people capable of living in that new environment.

What gave the first Christians this conviction? The answer is the Resurrection—and the great anticipation of the Resurrection, which is the Transfiguration. This ordinary Jesus somehow became transformed, elevated, enhanced in his manner of being.

The first thing we notice is that his appearance becomes more beautiful. These somewhat grubby bodies of ours are destined for a transfigured, elevated beauty.

Secondly, in his transfigured state, Jesus transcends space and time, since he is talking with Moses and Elijah. In this world, we are caught in one moment of space and time, but in heaven, we will live in the eternal now of God's life.

Have you ever noticed that even as we appreciate all that is wonderful about this life, we are never really at home? There is a permanent restlessness about human life. But a higher, richer, more beautiful and spiritually fulfilling life awaits us.

Reflect: How often do you reflect on *theosis* or deification—our becoming divine in and through Christ? Where in the Catholic faith do you see this deifying purpose?

MARCH 2, 2026

Monday of the Second Week of Lent

Luke 6:36–38

Jesus said to his disciples: "Be merciful, just as your Father is merciful.

"Stop judging and you will not be judged. Stop condemning and you will not be condemned. Forgive and you will be forgiven. Give and gifts will be given to you; a good measure, packed together, shaken down, and overflowing, will be poured into your lap. For the measure with which you measure will in return be measured out to you."

Friends, in today's Gospel, Jesus charges us to be merciful and to stop judging others. But we cannot perform such behaviors on our own strength—we need God's assistance.

In the Sermon on the Mount in Matthew, Jesus tells his followers, "Be perfect, just as your heavenly Father is perfect." The perfection that he urges—which includes a radical love of enemies, the practice of nonviolence in the face of aggression, the refusal to judge one's brothers and sisters, and an embrace of poverty, meekness, and simplicity of heart—is not desirable or even possible within a natural framework.

The form of life outlined in the Sermon on the Mount would strike Aristotle as excessive and irrational—and that is just the point. Its viability and beauty will emerge only when one's mind, will, and body have been invaded and elevated by the love that God is.

This is not to say that the natural moral excellences perceived by Aristotle are invalidated by grace; the invasion of the sacred does not overwhelm or undermine the secular. But it does indeed transfigure it. This transfiguration is the effect of love, working its way through the moral self.

Reflect: How have you allowed the inrushing of faith, hope, and love—the life of Jesus within you—to transfigure your own natural moral form?

MARCH 3, 2026

Tuesday of the Second Week of Lent

Matthew 23:1–12

Jesus spoke to the crowds and to his disciples, saying, "The scribes and the Pharisees have taken their seat on the chair of Moses. Therefore, do and observe all things whatsoever they tell you, but do not follow their example. For they preach but they do not practice. They tie up heavy burdens hard to carry and lay them on people's shoulders, but they will not lift a finger to move them. All their works are performed to be seen. They widen their phylacteries and lengthen their tassels. They love places of honor at banquets, seats of honor in synagogues, greetings in marketplaces, and the salutation 'Rabbi.' As for you, do not be called 'Rabbi.' You have but one teacher, and you are all brothers. Call no one on earth your father; you have but one Father in heaven. Do not be called 'Master'; you have but one master, the Christ. The greatest among you must be your servant. Whoever exalts himself will be humbled; but whoever humbles himself will be exalted."

Friends, in today's Gospel, Jesus turns his sharp eye and withering critique on the many ways that religious leaders fall into corruption. What precisely is bothering Jesus? Some religious leaders get their kicks from burdening people, laying the law on them heavily, making demands that are terrible, exulting in their own moral superiority.

At the core of Jesus' program is a willingness to bear other people's burdens, to help them carry their loads. And this applies to the moral life as well. If we lay the burden of God's law on people, we must be willing, at the same time, to help them bear it.

Another classic problem with religious people and especially religious leaders: they use the law and morality as a means of inflating the ego. The trouble is that this drug wears off rather quickly, and then we want more of it. We need a greater title, more respect, more recognition.

What is Jesus' recommendation for those caught in this dilemma? To be great is to be a servant: lowly, simple, often forgotten. Eschew marks of respect; don't seek them. Be satisfied with doing your work, whatever it is, on behalf of God's kingdom.

Reflect: Where in your spiritual life do you find the temptation to remain locked in the prison of your own egotism, looking at yourself rather than exploring the infinite mystery of God?

MARCH 4, 2026

Wednesday of the Second Week of Lent

Matthew 20:17–28

As Jesus was going up to Jerusalem, he took the Twelve disciples aside by themselves, and said to them on the way, "Behold, we are going up to Jerusalem, and the Son of Man will be handed over to the chief priests and the scribes, and they will condemn him to death, and hand him over to the Gentiles to be mocked and scourged and crucified, and he will be raised on the third day."

Then the mother of the sons of Zebedee approached Jesus with her sons and did him homage, wishing to ask him for something. He said to her, "What do you wish?" She answered him, "Command that these two sons of mine sit, one at your right and the other at your left, in your kingdom." Jesus said in reply, "You do not know what you are asking. Can you drink the chalice that I am going to drink?" They said to him, "We can." He replied, "My chalice you will indeed drink, but to sit at my right and at my left, this is not mine to give but is for those for whom it has been prepared by my Father." When the ten heard this, they became indignant at the two brothers. But Jesus summoned them and said, "You know that the rulers of the Gentiles lord it over them, and the great ones make their authority over them felt. But it shall not be so among you. Rather, whoever wishes to be great among you shall be your servant; whoever wishes to be first among you shall be your slave. Just so, the Son of Man did not come to be served but to serve and to give his life as a ransom for many."

Friends, in today's Gospel, the mother of James and John asks Jesus on their behalf to place them in high places in his kingdom. They are asking for two of the classic four substitutes for God: wealth, pleasure, power, and honor. The two brothers specifically want the last two.

Power is not, in itself, a bad thing. And the same is true of honor. Thomas Aquinas said that honor is the flag of virtue. It's a way of signaling to others something that's worth noticing.

So then what's the problem? The problem is that they are asking for these two things in the wrong spirit. The ego will want to use power, not for God's purposes or in service of truth, beauty, and goodness, but for its own aggrandizement and defense. When honor is sought for its own sake or in order to puff up the ego, it becomes dangerous as well.

What's the way out? Jesus tells us: "Whoever wishes to be great among you shall be your servant; whoever wishes to be first among you shall be your slave." When you serve others, when you become the least, you are accessing the power of God and seeking the honor of God.

Reflect: When in your life have you become manipulative, overbearing, and cruel in the pursuit of power? When have you become drunk on recognition, titles, and privileges in seeking honor for its own sake?

MARCH 5, 2026

Thursday of the Second Week of Lent

Luke 16:19–31

Jesus said to the Pharisees: "There was a rich man who dressed in purple garments and fine linen and dined sumptuously each day. And lying at his door was a poor man named Lazarus, covered with sores, who would gladly have eaten his fill of the scraps that fell from the rich man's table. Dogs even used to come and lick his sores. When the poor man died, he was carried away by angels to the bosom of Abraham. The rich man also died and was buried, and from the netherworld, where he was in torment, he raised his eyes and saw Abraham far off and Lazarus at his side. And he cried out, 'Father Abraham, have pity on me. Send Lazarus to dip the tip of his finger in water and cool my tongue, for I am suffering torment in these flames.' Abraham replied, 'My child, remember that you received what was good during your lifetime while Lazarus likewise received what was bad; but now he is comforted here, whereas you are tormented. Moreover, between us and you a great chasm is established to prevent anyone from crossing who might wish to go from our side to yours or from your side to ours.' He said, 'Then I beg you, father, send him to my father's house, for I have five brothers, so that he may warn them, lest they too come to this place of torment.' But Abraham replied, 'They have Moses and the prophets. Let them listen to them.' He said, 'Oh no, father Abraham, but if someone from the dead goes to them, they will repent.' Then Abraham said, 'If they will not listen to Moses and the prophets, neither will they be persuaded if someone should rise from the dead.'"

Friends, today's Gospel reading is the story of the poor man Lazarus, who sat outside the door of a rich man and "would gladly have eaten his fill of the scraps that fell from the rich man's table." The rich man isn't named, and that's very interesting. In the ancient world, the rich and powerful were the ones who deserved to have their names mentioned. Whose names weren't mentioned? The poor and the marginalized. So this is a very interesting reversal that is going on here.

And we know this story well. Day after day, the rich man walks past Lazarus, in and out of his house. When Lazarus dies, he's taken to the "bosom of Abraham." But the rich man dies and he's taken to the underworld. Again another reversal. You'd expect that God has blessed the rich and powerful and cursed those who are poor and hopeless. But that's not the way the Bible imagines this situation. It's Lazarus who's carried to paradise and the rich man who's carried downward.

There's the revolutionary quality of the Bible, turning our expectations upside down.

Reflect: How much do you care for those who are poor? Can you name them, or are they for you, as for ancient peoples, just a nameless mass of suffering people? And are you committed to helping these people by performing the corporal works of mercy?

MARCH 6, 2026

Friday of the Second Week of Lent

Matthew 21:33–43, 45–46

Jesus said to the chief priests and the elders of the people: "Hear another parable. There was a landowner who planted a vineyard, put a hedge around it, dug a wine press in it, and built a tower. Then he leased it to tenants and went on a journey. When vintage time drew near, he sent his servants to the tenants to obtain his produce. But the tenants seized the servants and one they beat, another they killed, and a third they stoned. Again he sent other servants, more numerous than the first ones, but they treated them in the same way. Finally, he sent his son to them, thinking, 'They will respect my son.' But when the tenants saw the son, they said to one another, 'This is the heir. Come, let us kill him and acquire his inheritance.' They seized him, threw him out of the vineyard, and killed him. What will the owner of the vineyard do to those tenants when he comes?" They answered him, "He will put those wretched men to a wretched death and lease his vineyard to other tenants who will give him the produce at the proper times." Jesus said to them,

"Did you never read in the Scriptures:

The stone that the builders rejected
has become the cornerstone;
by the Lord has this been done,
and it is wonderful in our eyes?

Therefore, I say to you, the Kingdom of God will be taken away from you and given to a people that will produce its fruit." When the chief priests and the Pharisees heard his parables, they knew that he was speaking about them. And although they were attempting to arrest him, they feared the crowds, for they regarded him as a prophet.

Friends, just before his Passion and death, Jesus tells this striking story of the landowner who planted a vineyard. The fertile vineyard stands for Israel, his chosen people. But it could be broadened out to include the world. What do we learn from this beautiful image? That God has made for his people a place where they can find rest, enjoyment, and good work.

We—Israel, the Church, the world—are not the owners of this vineyard; we are tenants. One of the most fundamental spiritual mistakes we can make is to think that we own the world. We are tenants, entrusted with the responsibility of caring for it, but everything that we have and are is on loan. Our lives are not about us.

Christ is God's judgment. We are all under his judgment. In the measure that we reject him or refuse to listen to him, we place our tenancy in jeopardy. And so the great question that arises from this reading:

Reflect: How are you using the gifts that God gave you for God's purposes—your money, time, talents, creativity, relationships? Do you believe that all is for God, and thus all is under God's judgment?

MARCH 7, 2026

Saturday of the Second Week of Lent

Luke 15:1–3, 11–32

Tax collectors and sinners were all drawing near to listen to Jesus, but the Pharisees and scribes began to complain, saying, "This man welcomes sinners and eats with them." So to them Jesus addressed this parable. "A man had two sons, and the younger son said to his father, 'Father, give me the share of your estate that should come to me.' So the father divided the property between them. After a few days, the younger son collected all his belongings and set off to a distant country where he squandered his inheritance on a life of dissipation. When he had freely spent everything, a severe famine struck that country, and he found himself in dire need. So he hired himself out to one of the local citizens who sent him to his farm to tend the swine. And he longed to eat his fill of the pods on which the swine fed, but nobody gave him any. Coming to his senses he thought, 'How many of my father's hired workers have more than enough food to eat, but here am I, dying from hunger. I shall get up and go to my father and I shall say to him,

"Father, I have sinned against heaven and against you. I no longer deserve to be called your son; treat me as you would treat one of your hired workers."' So he got up and went back to his father. While he was still a long way off, his father caught sight of him, and was filled with compassion. He ran to his son, embraced him and kissed him. His son said to him, 'Father, I have sinned against heaven and against you; I no longer deserve to be called your son.' But his father ordered his servants, 'Quickly, bring the finest robe and put it on him; put a ring on his finger and sandals on his feet. Take the fattened calf and slaughter it. Then let us celebrate with a feast, because this son of mine was dead, and has come to life again; he was lost, and has been found.' Then the celebration began. Now the older son had been out in the field and, on his way back, as he neared the house, he heard the sound of music and dancing. He called one of the servants and asked what this might mean. The servant said to him, 'Your brother has returned and your father has slaughtered the fattened calf because he has him back safe and sound.' He became angry, and when he refused to enter the house, his father came out and pleaded with him. He said to his father in reply, 'Look, all these years I served you and not once did

I disobey your orders; yet you never gave me even a young goat to feast on with my friends. But when your son returns who swallowed up your property with prostitutes, for him you slaughter the fattened calf.' He said to him, 'My son, you are here with me always; everything I have is yours. But now we must celebrate and rejoice, because your brother was dead and has come to life again; he was lost and has been found.'"

Friends, at the core of today's Gospel is a portrait of our God, who is prodigal. The father stands for the God whose very nature is to give, the God who simply *is* love. And the younger son stands for all of us sinners who tend to misunderstand how to access the divine love.

Since God exists only in gift form, his life, even in principle, cannot become a possession. Instead, it is "had" only on the fly, only in the measure that it is given away. When we cling to it, it disappears, according to a kind of spiritual physics.

The Greek that lies behind "distant country" in the parable is *chora makra*; that means, literally, "the great emptiness." Trying to turn the divine gift into the ego's possession necessarily results in nothing, nonbeing, the void.

Pope St. John Paul II formulated the principle here as "the law of the gift"—that your being increases inasmuch as you give it away. If clinging and possessing are the marks of the *chora makra*, then the law of the gift is the defining dynamic of the father's house, where the robe and the ring and the fatted calf are on permanent offer.

Reflect: In what ways do you try to cling to God's life and make of it your own possession? How can you practice the law of the gift and instead give it away?

MARCH 8, 2026

Third Sunday of Lent

John 4:5–42 (or 4:5–15, 19b–26, 39a, 40–42)

Jesus came to a town of Samaria called Sychar, near the plot of land that Jacob had given to his son Joseph. Jacob's well was there. Jesus, tired from his journey, sat down there at the well. It was about noon.

A woman of Samaria came to draw water. Jesus said to her, "Give me a drink." His disciples had gone into the town to buy food. The Samaritan woman said to him, "How can you, a Jew, ask me, a Samaritan woman, for a drink?"—For Jews use nothing in common with Samaritans.—Jesus answered and said to her, "If you knew the gift of God and who is saying to you, 'Give me a drink,' you would have asked him and he would have given you living water." The woman said to him, "Sir, you do not even have a bucket and the cistern is deep; where then can you get this living water? Are you greater than our father Jacob, who gave us this cistern and drank from it himself with his children and his flocks?" Jesus answered and said to her, "Everyone who drinks this water will be thirsty again; but whoever drinks the water I shall give will never thirst; the water I shall give will become in him a spring of water welling up to eternal life." The woman said to him, "Sir, give me this water, so that I may not be thirsty or have to keep coming here to draw water."

Jesus said to her, "Go call your husband and come back." The woman answered and said to him, "I do not have a husband." Jesus answered her, "You are right in saying, 'I do not have a husband.' For you have had five husbands, and the one you have now is not your husband. What you have said is true." The woman said to him, "Sir, I can see that you are a prophet. Our ancestors worshiped on this mountain; but you people say that the place to worship is in Jerusalem." Jesus said to her, "Believe me, woman, the hour is coming when you will worship the Father neither on this mountain nor in Jerusalem. You people worship what you do not understand; we worship what we understand, because salvation is from the Jews. But the hour is coming, and is now here, when true worshipers will worship the Father in Spirit and truth; and indeed the Father seeks such people to worship him. God is Spirit, and those who worship him must worship in Spirit and truth." The woman said to him, "I know that the Messiah is coming, the one called the Christ; when he comes, he will tell us everything." Jesus said to her, "I am he, the one speaking with you."

At that moment his disciples returned, and were amazed that he was talking with a woman, but still no one said, "What are you looking for?" or "Why are you talking with her?" The woman left her water jar and went into the town and said to the people, "Come see a man who told me everything I have done. Could he possibly be the Christ?" They went out of the town and came to him. Meanwhile, the disciples urged him, "Rabbi, eat." But he said to them, "I have food to eat of which you do not know." So the disciples said to one another, "Could someone have brought him something to eat?" Jesus said to them, "My food is to do the will of the one who sent me and to finish his work. Do you not say, 'In four months the harvest will be here'? I tell you, look up and see the fields ripe for the harvest. The reaper is already receiving payment and gathering crops for eternal life, so that the sower and reaper can rejoice together. For here the saying is verified that 'One sows and another reaps.' I sent you to reap what you have not worked for; others have done the work, and you are sharing the fruits of their work."

Many of the Samaritans of that town began to believe in him because of the word of the woman who testified, "He told me everything I have done." When the Samaritans came to him, they invited him to stay with them; and he stayed there two days. Many more began to believe in him because of his word, and they said to the woman, "We no longer believe because of your word; for we have heard for ourselves, and we know that this is truly the savior of the world."

Friends, today we read the magnificent story from John's Gospel about the woman at the well. The image of thirst is used throughout the Bible to speak of the human longing for God.

At the height of the heat of the day, Jesus asks a Samaritan woman for a drink of water. We are on very holy ground, for the whole of salvation is summed up here: our thirst for God meets God's even more dramatic thirst for us. Augustine picked up on this in his commentary on the passage: "Jesus was thirsty for the woman's faith."

At first, of course, the woman is put off. How could this Jewish man be asking me for a drink? Translate this into spiritual language: How could almighty God be thirsty for my faith and my attention?

Jesus' answer is magnificent: "Everyone who drinks this water will be thirsty again; but whoever drinks the water I shall give will never thirst." We are built for union with God, and therefore we thirst for God with an infinite desire. What Jesus offers her is the life of grace, the divine life, God's own self. That's the only energy that can ever satisfy our infinite longing.

Reflect: Have you ever hooked your infinite desire onto something or someone less than God? When you came back to that well over and over again, what happened?

MARCH 9, 2026

Monday of the Third Week of Lent

Luke 4:24–30

Jesus said to the people in the synagogue at Nazareth: "Amen, I say to you, no prophet is accepted in his own native place. Indeed, I tell you, there were many widows in Israel in the days of Elijah when the sky was closed for three and a half years and a severe famine spread over the entire land. It was to none of these that Elijah was sent, but only to a widow in Zarephath in the land of Sidon. Again, there were many lepers in Israel during the time of Elisha the prophet; yet not one of them was cleansed, but only Naaman the Syrian." When the people in the synagogue heard this, they were all filled with fury. They rose up, drove him out of the town, and led him to the brow of the hill on which their town had been built, to hurl him down headlong. But he passed through the midst of them and went away.

Friends, in today's Gospel, Jesus' hometown rejects him as a prophet. And I want to say a word about your role as a prophet.

When most laypeople hear about prophecy, they sit back and their eyes glaze over. "That's something for the priests and the bishops to worry about; they're the modern-day prophets. I don't have that call or that responsibility."

Well, think again! Vatican II emphasized the universal call to holiness, rooted in the dynamics of Baptism. Every baptized person is conformed unto Christ—priest, prophet, and king. Whenever you assist at Mass, you are exercising your priestly office, participating in the worship of God. Whenever you direct your kids to discover their mission in the Church, or provide guidance to someone in the spiritual life, you are exercising your kingly office.

As a baptized individual, you are commissioned as a prophet—which is to say, a speaker of God's truth. And the prophetic word is not your own. It is not the result of your own meditations on the spiritual life, as valuable and correct as those may be. The prophetic word is the word of God given to you by God.

Reflect: Speaking prophetically means that the words of God are on your lips regularly. How often do you read the Bible? Do you listen attentively at Mass to the proclamation and preaching of the biblical Word?

MARCH 10, 2026

Tuesday of the Third Week of Lent

Matthew 18:21–35

Peter approached Jesus and asked him, "Lord, if my brother sins against me, how often must I forgive him? As many as seven times?" Jesus answered, "I say to you, not seven times but seventy-seven times. That is why the Kingdom of heaven may be likened to a king who decided to settle accounts with his servants. When he began the accounting, a debtor was brought before him who owed him a huge amount. Since he had no way of paying it back, his master ordered him to be sold, along with his wife, his children, and all his property, in payment of the debt. At that, the servant fell down, did him homage, and said, 'Be patient with me, and I will pay you back in full.' Moved with compassion the master of that servant let him go and forgave him the loan. When that servant had left, he found one of his fellow servants who owed him a much smaller amount. He seized him and started to choke him, demanding, 'Pay back what you owe.' Falling to his knees, his fellow servant begged him, 'Be patient with me, and I will pay you back.' But he refused. Instead, he had him put in prison until he paid back the debt. Now when his fellow servants saw what had happened, they were deeply disturbed, and went to their master and reported the whole affair. His master summoned him and said to him, 'You wicked servant! I forgave you your entire debt because you begged me to. Should you not have had pity on your fellow servant, as I had pity on you?' Then in anger his master handed him over to the torturers until he should pay back the whole debt. So will my heavenly Father do to you, unless each of you forgives your brother from your heart."

Friends, in today's Gospel, Jesus tells a parable that illustrates God's mercy. The Latin word for mercy is *misericordia*, which designates the suffering of the heart, or compassion—*cum patior* ("I suffer with").

Mercy is identical to what the Old Testament authors refer to as God's *hesed*, or tender mercy. It is *the* characteristic of God, for God is love. The love that obtains among the Trinitarian persons spills over into God's love for the world that he has made.

Think of a mother's love for her children. Could you ever imagine a mother becoming indifferent to one of her offspring? But even should she forget, we read in the prophet Isaiah, God will never forget his own. Consider the fact that nothing would exist were it not willed into being by God. But God has no need of anything; hence, his sustaining of the universe is an act of disinterested love and tender mercy.

There is no greater manifestation of the divine mercy than the forgiveness of sins. When G.K. Chesterton was asked why he became a Catholic, he answered, "To have my sins forgiven." This is the greatest grace the Church can offer: reconciliation, the restoration of the divine friendship, the forgiveness of our sins.

Reflect: Why has confession fallen into disuse in recent decades? How often do you receive and feel God's mercy through the sacrament of reconciliation?

MARCH 11, 2026

Wednesday of the Third Week of Lent

Matthew 5:17–19

Jesus said to his disciples: "Do not think that I have come to abolish the law or the prophets. I have come not to abolish but to fulfill. Amen, I say to you, until heaven and earth pass away, not the smallest letter or the smallest part of a letter will pass from the law, until all things have taken place. Therefore, whoever breaks one of the least of these commandments and teaches others to do so will be called least in the Kingdom of heaven. But whoever obeys and teaches these commandments will be called greatest in the Kingdom of heaven."

Friends, in our Gospel today, Jesus declares that he would not undermine the Law and the prophets, but fulfill them. Jesus himself was an observant Jew, and the themes and images of the Holy Scriptures were elemental for him.

But what is he going to fulfill? Protestant theologian N.T. Wright has pointed out that the Old Testament is essentially an unfinished symphony, a drama without a climax. It is the articulation of a hope, a dream, a longing—but without a realization of that hope, without a satisfaction of that longing.

Israel knew itself to be the people with the definite mission to become holy and thereby to render the world holy. But instead, Israel fell into greater and greater sins, and instead of being the catalyst for the conversion of the world, the world was continually overwhelming and enslaving Israel.

And then came Jesus, who turned out to be, in the most unexpected way, the fulfillment of the dream. From the beginning of his ministry, Jesus effected the gathering of the tribes of Israel through conversion and the forgiveness of sins.

Reflect: All of those social and religious conventions that had effectively divided Israel, Jesus sought to overcome and expose as fraudulent. What social conventions divide the new Israel, the Church, today? How can you, like Jesus, reach out to everyone—rich and poor, healthy and sick, saints and sinners?

MARCH 12, 2026

Thursday of the Third Week of Lent

Luke 11:14–23

Jesus was driving out a demon that was mute, and when the demon had gone out, the mute man spoke and the crowds were amazed. Some of them said, "By the power of Beelzebul, the prince of demons, he drives out demons." Others, to test him, asked him for a sign from heaven. But he knew their thoughts and said to them, "Every kingdom divided against itself will be laid waste and house will fall against house. And if Satan is divided against himself, how will his kingdom stand? For you say that it is by Beelzebul that I drive out demons. If I, then, drive out demons by Beelzebul, by whom do your own people drive them out? Therefore they will be your judges. But if it is by the finger of God that I drive out demons, then the Kingdom of God has come upon you. When a strong man fully armed guards his palace, his possessions are safe. But when one stronger than he attacks and overcomes him, he takes away the armor on which he relied and distributes the spoils. Whoever is not with me is against me, and whoever does not gather with me scatters."

Friends, in today's Gospel, we learn of a person possessed by a demon. Jesus meets the man and drives out the demon, but then is immediately accused of being in league with Satan. Some of the witnesses said, "By the power of Beelzebul, the prince of demons, he drives out demons."

Jesus' response is wonderful in its logic and laconicism: "Every kingdom divided against itself will be laid waste and house will fall against house. And if Satan is divided against himself, how will his kingdom stand?"

The demonic power is always one of scattering. It breaks up communion. But Jesus, as always, is the voice of *communio*, of one bringing things back together.

Think back to Jesus' feeding of the five thousand. Facing a large, hungry crowd, his disciples beg him to "dismiss the crowds so that they can go to the villages and buy food for themselves." But Jesus answers, "There is no need for them to go away; give them some food yourselves."

Whatever drives the Church apart is an echo of this "dismiss the crowds" impulse and a reminder of the demonic tendency to divide. In times of trial and threat, this is a very common instinct. We blame, attack, break up, and disperse. But Jesus is right: "There is no need for them to go away."

Reflect: How often do you perceive a problem in the Church but then abdicate responsibility for it? What can you offer to Jesus, in an attitude of love, to create and sustain the *communio* of the Church—even the very little you have?

MARCH 13, 2026

Friday of the Third Week of Lent

Mark 12:28–34

One of the scribes came to Jesus and asked him, "Which is the first of all the commandments?" Jesus replied, "The first is this:

Hear, O Israel!

The Lord our God is Lord alone!

You shall love the Lord your God with all your heart,
with all your soul,
with all your mind,
and with all your strength.

The second is this:

You shall love your neighbor as yourself.

There is no other commandment greater than these." The scribe said to him, "Well said, teacher. You are right in saying,

He is One and there is no other than he.

And *to love him with all your heart,*
with all your understanding,
with all your strength,
and to love your neighbor as yourself

is worth more than all burnt offerings and sacrifices." And when Jesus saw that he answered with understanding, he said to him, "You are not far from the Kingdom of God." And no one dared to ask him any more questions.

Friends, in today's Gospel, Jesus sums up the laws of love.

It was a common practice in Jesus' time to ask a rabbi to identify the central precept of the Law. Thus Jesus is asked, "Which is the first of all the commandments?"

He gave his famous answer: "'You shall love the Lord your God with all your heart, with all your soul, with all your mind, and with all your strength.' The second is this: 'You shall love your neighbor as yourself.'"

All of religion is finally about awakening the deepest desire of the heart and directing it toward God; it is about the ordering of love toward that which is most worthy of love. But this love of God carries, Jesus says, as a necessary implication, compassion for one's fellow human beings.

Why are the two commandments so tightly linked? Because of who Jesus is. Christ is not simply a human being, and he is not simply God; rather, he is the God-man, the one in whose person divinity and humanity meet. Therefore, it is impossible to love him as God without loving the humanity that he has embraced. The greatest commandment is, therefore, an indirect Christology.

Reflect: Where, in the lives of the saints, do you find this entwined love of God and neighbor?

MARCH 14, 2026

Saturday of the Third Week of Lent

Luke 18:9–14

Jesus addressed this parable to those who were convinced of their own righteousness and despised everyone else. "Two people went up to the temple area to pray; one was a Pharisee and the other was a tax collector. The Pharisee took up his position and spoke this prayer to himself, 'O God, I thank you that I am not like the rest of humanity—greedy, dishonest, adulterous—or even like this tax collector. I fast twice a week, and I pay tithes on my whole income.' But the tax collector stood off at a distance and would not even raise his eyes to heaven but beat his breast and prayed, 'O God, be merciful to me a sinner.' I tell you, the latter went home justified, not the former; for everyone who exalts himself will be humbled, and the one who humbles himself will be exalted."

Friends, today's Gospel compares the self-centered prayer of the Pharisee with the God-centered prayer of the tax collector.

The Pharisee spoke his prayer to himself. This is, Jesus suggests, a fraudulent, wholly inadequate prayer, precisely because it simply confirms the man in his self-regard. And the god to which he prays is, necessarily, a false god, an idol, since it allows itself to be positioned by the ego-driven needs of the Pharisee.

But then Jesus invites us to meditate upon the publican's prayer. He speaks with a simple eloquence: "[He] beat his breast and prayed, 'O God, be merciful to me a sinner.'" Though it is articulate speech, it is not language that confirms the independence and power of the speaker—just the contrary. It is more of a cry or a groan, an acknowledgment that he needs to receive something, this mysterious mercy for which he begs.

In the first prayer, "god" is the principal member of the audience arrayed before the ego of the Pharisee. But in this second prayer, God is the principal actor, and the publican is the audience awaiting a performance the contours of which he cannot fully foresee.

Reflect: Some of the most powerful prayers are simple, unadorned, even blunt. How often do you pray in this way?

MARCH 15, 2026

Fourth Sunday of Lent

John 9:1–41 (or 9:1, 6–9, 13–17, 34–38)

As Jesus passed by he saw a man blind from birth. His disciples asked him, "Rabbi, who sinned, this man or his parents, that he was born blind?" Jesus answered, "Neither he nor his parents sinned; it is so that the works of God might be made visible through him. We have to do the works of the one who sent me while it is day. Night is coming when no one can work. While I am in the world, I am the light of the world." When he had said this, he spat on the ground and made clay with the saliva, and smeared the clay on his eyes, and said to him, "Go wash in the Pool of Siloam"—which means Sent—. So he went and washed, and came back able to see.

His neighbors and those who had seen him earlier as a beggar said, "Isn't this the one who used to sit and beg?" Some said, "It is," but others said, "No, he just looks like him." He said, "I am." So they said to him, "How were your eyes opened?" He replied, "The man called Jesus made clay and anointed my eyes and told me, 'Go to Siloam and wash.' So I went there and washed and was able to see." And they said to him, "Where is he?" He said, "I don't know."

They brought the one who was once blind to the Pharisees. Now Jesus had made clay and opened his eyes on a sabbath. So then the Pharisees also asked him how he was able to see. He said to them, "He put clay on my eyes, and I washed, and now I can see." So some of the Pharisees said, "This man is not from God, because he does not keep the sabbath." But others said, "How can a sinful man do such signs?" And there was a division among them. So they said to the blind man again, "What do you have to say about him, since he opened your eyes?" He said, "He is a prophet."

Now the Jews did not believe that he had been blind and gained his sight until they summoned the parents of the one who had gained his sight. They asked them, "Is this your son, who you say was born blind? How does he now see?" His parents answered and said, "We know that this is our son and that he was born blind. We do not know how he sees now, nor do we know who opened his eyes. Ask him, he is of age; he can speak for himself." His parents said this because they were afraid of the Jews, for the Jews had already agreed that if anyone acknowledged him as the Christ, he would be expelled from the synagogue. For this reason his parents said, "He is of age; question him."

So a second time they called the man who had been blind and said to him, "Give God the praise! We know that this man is a sinner." He replied, "If he is a sinner, I do not know. One thing I do know is that I was blind and now I see." So they said to him, "What did he do to you? How did he open your eyes?" He answered them, "I told you already and you did not listen. Why do you want to hear it again? Do you want to become his disciples, too?" They ridiculed him and said, "You are that man's disciple; we are disciples of Moses! We know that God spoke to Moses, but we do not know where this one is from." The man answered and said to them, "This is what is so amazing, that you do not know where he is from, yet he opened my eyes. We know that God does not listen to sinners, but if one is devout and does his will, he listens to him. It is unheard of that anyone ever opened the eyes of a person born blind. If this man were not from God, he would not be able to do anything." They answered and said to him, "You were born totally in sin, and are you trying to teach us?" Then they threw him out.

When Jesus heard that they had thrown him out, he found him and said, "Do you believe in the Son of Man?" He answered and said, "Who is he, sir, that I may believe in him?" Jesus said to him, "You have seen him, the one speaking with you is he." He said, "I do believe, Lord," and he worshiped him. Then Jesus said, "I came into this world for judgment, so that those who do not see might see, and those who do see might become blind."

Some of the Pharisees who were with him heard this and said to him, "Surely we are not also blind, are we?" Jesus said to them, "If you were blind, you would have no sin; but now you are saying, 'We see,' so your sin remains."

Friends, today in the strange and strikingly beautiful account of the healing of the man born blind in John's Gospel, we find an iconic representation of Christianity as a way of *seeing*. Jesus spits on the ground and makes a mud paste, which he then rubs onto the man's eyes. When the man washes his eyes in the pool of Siloam as Jesus had instructed him, his sight is restored.

The crowds are amazed, but the Pharisees—consternated and skeptical—accuse him of being naïve and the one who healed him of being a sinner. With disarming simplicity the visionary responds, "If he is a sinner, I do not know. One thing I do know is that I was blind and now I see."

This is precisely what all Christians say when they have encountered the light of Christ. It was St. Augustine who saw in the making of the mud paste a metaphor for the Incarnation: the divine power mixing with the earth, resulting in the formation of a healing balm. When this salve of God made flesh is rubbed onto our eyes blinded by sin, we come again to see.

Reflect: How have you come to vision through Christ?

MARCH 16, 2026

Monday of the Fourth Week of Lent

John 4:43–54

At that time Jesus left [Samaria] for Galilee. For Jesus himself testified that a prophet has no honor in his native place. When he came into Galilee, the Galileans welcomed him, since they had seen all he had done in Jerusalem at the feast; for they themselves had gone to the feast.

Then he returned to Cana in Galilee, where he had made the water wine. Now there was a royal official whose son was ill in Capernaum. When he heard that Jesus had arrived in Galilee from Judea, he went to him and asked him to come down and heal his son, who was near death. Jesus said to him, "Unless you people see signs and wonders, you will not believe." The royal official said to him, "Sir, come down before my child dies." Jesus said to him, "You may go; your son will live." The man believed what Jesus said to him and left. While the man was on his way back, his slaves met him and told him that his boy would live. He asked them when he began to recover. They told him, "The fever left him yesterday, about one in the afternoon." The father realized that just at that time Jesus had said to him, "Your son will live," and he and his whole household came to believe. Now this was the second sign Jesus did when he came to Galilee from Judea.

Friends, in today's Gospel, Jesus heals the son of a royal official.

Healer: that's why he's come; that's who he is. In Jesus, divinity and humanity meet. His hands and mouth and his eyes, his whole body becomes a conduit of God's energy. What's God's energy, God's purpose? To set right a world gone wrong, a suffering world. Out of every pore of his body, Jesus expresses the healing love of God.

Jesus' ministry of healing expresses in history God's ultimate intention for the world. In Jesus we see a hint of that world to come where there will be no more suffering, no more sadness, no more sickness.

He does not wait for the sinner, the sufferer, the marginalized to come to him. In love and humility, he goes to them. This same Jesus, risen from the dead, present and alive in the Church, is still seeking us out, coming into our homes—not waiting for us to crawl to him, but seeking us out in love and humility.

Reflect: How have you experienced the healing power of Jesus?

MARCH 17, 2026

Tuesday of the Fourth Week of Lent

John 5:1–16

There was a feast of the Jews, and Jesus went up to Jerusalem. Now there is in Jerusalem at the Sheep Gate a pool called in Hebrew Bethesda, with five porticoes. In these lay a large number of ill, blind, lame, and crippled. One man was there who had been ill for thirty-eight years. When Jesus saw him lying there and knew that he had been ill for a long time, he said to him, "Do you want to be well?" The sick man answered him, "Sir, I have no one to put me into the pool when the water is stirred up; while I am on my way, someone else gets down there before me." Jesus said to him, "Rise, take up your mat, and walk." Immediately the man became well, took up his mat, and walked.

Now that day was a sabbath. So the Jews said to the man who was cured, "It is the sabbath, and it is not lawful for you to carry your mat." He answered them, "The man who made me well told me, 'Take up your mat and walk.'" They asked him, "Who is the man who told you, 'Take it up and walk'?" The man who was healed did not know who it was, for Jesus had slipped away, since there was a crowd there. After this Jesus found him in the temple area and said to him, "Look, you are well; do not sin any more, so that nothing worse may happen to you." The man went and told the Jews that Jesus was the one who had made him well. Therefore, the Jews began to persecute Jesus because he did this on a sabbath.

Friends, in today's Gospel, we find the beautiful healing of a paralyzed man who had been ill for thirty-eight years. Jesus sees the man lying on his mat, next to a pool, and asks, "Do you want to be well?" The man answers him, and Jesus replies, "Rise, take up your mat, and walk." Immediately, the man is healed.

Now at this point, the story really heats up. We notice something that is frequently on display in the Gospels: the resistance to the creative work of God, the attempt to find any excuse, however lame, to deny it, to pretend it's not there, to condemn it.

One would expect that everyone around the cured man would rejoice, but just the contrary: the Jewish leaders are infuriated and confounded. They see the healed man, and their first response is, "It is the sabbath, and it is not lawful for you to carry your mat."

Why are they so reactive? Why don't they want this to be? We sinners don't like the ways of God. We find them troubling and threatening. Why? Because they undermine the games of oppression and exclusion that we rely upon in order to boost our own egos.

Let this encounter remind us that God's ways are not our ways, and that there is one even greater than the sabbath.

Reflect: It is in the interest of "in" groups that there be "out" groups. Are there certain groups of people that you would exclude from the joy of being healed by Christ?

MARCH 18, 2026

Wednesday of the Fourth Week of Lent

John 5:17–30

Jesus answered the Jews: "My Father is at work until now, so I am at work." For this reason they tried all the more to kill him, because he not only broke the sabbath but he also called God his own father, making himself equal to God.

Jesus answered and said to them, "Amen, amen, I say to you, the Son cannot do anything on his own, but only what he sees the Father doing; for what he does, the Son will do also. For the Father loves the Son and shows him everything that he himself does, and he will show him greater works than these, so that you may be amazed. For just as the Father raises the dead and gives life, so also does the Son give life to whomever he wishes. Nor does the Father judge anyone, but he has given all judgment to the Son, so that all may honor the Son just as they honor the Father. Whoever does not honor the Son does not honor the Father who sent him. Amen, amen, I say to you, whoever hears my word and believes in the one who sent me has eternal life and will not come to condemnation, but has passed from death to life. Amen, amen, I say to you, the hour is coming and is now here when the dead will hear the voice of the Son of God, and those who hear will live. For just as the Father has life in himself, so also he gave to the Son the possession of life in himself. And he gave him power to exercise judgment, because he is the Son of Man. Do not be amazed at this, because the hour is coming in which all who are in the tombs will hear his voice and will come out, those who have done good deeds to the resurrection of life, but those who have done wicked deeds to the resurrection of condemnation.

"I cannot do anything on my own; I judge as I hear, and my judgment is just, because I do not seek my own will but the will of the one who sent me."

Friends, in today's Gospel, we see Jesus as the judge who shows mercy and love.

The New Testament sense is that the suffering of the world is produced by the breaking of the loop of grace, the insistence that one's life should be one's own. When this attitude dominates, when we want knowledge of good and evil for ourselves, when we want what is coming to us, we end up losing the little that we think we have.

Jesus saved us by the whole course of his obedience. His life was an obedient response to the will of God, a displacement of his own concerns in favor of the Father's: "Amen, amen, I say to you, a Son cannot do anything on his own, but only what he sees his Father doing; for what he does, his Son will do also."

Reflect: In what ways are you willing to live in grace, commending your life to the Father in the confidence that he will return it to you? In what ways do you resist this loop of grace?

MARCH 19, 2026

Solemnity of Saint Joseph, Spouse of the Blessed Virgin Mary

Matthew 1:16, 18–21, 24a (or Luke 2:41–51a)

Jacob was the father of Joseph, the husband of Mary. Of her was born Jesus who is called the Christ.

Now this is how the birth of Jesus Christ came about. When his mother Mary was betrothed to Joseph, but before they lived together, she was found with child through the Holy Spirit. Joseph her husband, since he was a righteous man, yet unwilling to expose her to shame, decided to divorce her quietly. Such was his intention when, behold, the angel of the Lord appeared to him in a dream and said, "Joseph, son of David, do not be afraid to take Mary your wife into your home. For it is through the Holy Spirit that this child has been conceived in her. She will bear a son and you are to name him Jesus, because he will save his people from their sins." When Joseph awoke, he did as the angel of the Lord had commanded him and took his wife into his home.

Friends, on this feast of St. Joseph, our Gospel focuses on some powerful spiritual themes, all of which surround the birth of Jesus.

First, we look at the sadness and the quandary of Joseph. He had become betrothed to Mary, and then he finds that his betrothed is pregnant. So the engagement has to be called off because of an irregular pregnancy. This must have pained him at the deepest emotional level: the feeling of betrayal by one he had loved. It is a wonderful tribute to the goodness of Joseph that he didn't vent his frustration. Instead, he looked to the feelings of Mary, resolving to divorce her quietly.

Still, this must have been a spiritual crisis for him. What does God want him to do? Then the angel appears to him in a dream and tells him to take Mary as his wife. Joseph realizes that these puzzling events are part of God's much greater plan. He was willing to cooperate with the divine plan, though he in no way knew its contours or its deepest purposes. Like Mary at the Annunciation, he trusted and let himself be led.

Reflect: What appears to be a disaster from Joseph's perspective is meaningful from God's perspective. Have you ever experienced a crisis that you later realized was part of the greater plan of God?

MARCH 20, 2026

Friday of the Fourth Week of Lent

John 7:1–2, 10, 25–30

Jesus moved about within Galilee; he did not wish to travel in Judea, because the Jews were trying to kill him. But the Jewish feast of Tabernacles was near.

But when his brothers had gone up to the feast, he himself also went up, not openly but as it were in secret.

Some of the inhabitants of Jerusalem said, "Is he not the one they are trying to kill? And look, he is speaking openly and they say nothing to him. Could the authorities have realized that he is the Christ? But we know where he is from. When the Christ comes, no one will know where he is from." So Jesus cried out in the temple area as he was teaching and said, "You know me and also know where I am from. Yet I did not come on my own, but the one who sent me, whom you do not know, is true. I know him, because I am from him, and he sent me." So they tried to arrest him, but no one laid a hand upon him, because his hour had not yet come.

Friends, the Gospel for today centers around a theme that we can never speak of enough: the divinity of Jesus. There has been a disturbing tendency in recent years—you can see it clearly in Eckhart Tolle's bestselling book *The Power of Now*—to turn Jesus into an inspiring spiritual teacher, like the Buddha or the Sufi mystics.

But if that's all he is, the heck with him. The Gospels are never content with such a reductive description. Though they present Jesus quite clearly as a teacher, they know that he is infinitely more than that. They affirm that something else is at stake in him and in our relation to him.

In our Gospel today, Jesus plainly declares his relationship with his Father: "I did not come on my own, but the one who sent me, whom you do not know, is true. I know him, because I am from him, and he sent me."

Reflect: As the Church makes its way through stormy waters, only the divine Christ can assure us, "Be not afraid." Do you sometimes look for this assurance instead in a politician, activist, philosopher, teacher, or physician?

MARCH 21, 2026

Saturday of the Fourth Week of Lent

John 7:40–53

Some in the crowd who heard these words of Jesus said, "This is truly the Prophet." Others said, "This is the Christ." But others said, "The Christ will not come from Galilee, will he? Does not Scripture say that the Christ will be of David's family and come from Bethlehem, the village where David lived?" So a division occurred in the crowd because of him. Some of them even wanted to arrest him, but no one laid hands on him.

So the guards went to the chief priests and Pharisees, who asked them, "Why did you not bring him?" The guards answered, "Never before has anyone spoken like this man." So the Pharisees answered them, "Have you also been deceived? Have any of the authorities or the Pharisees believed in him? But this crowd, which does not know the law, is accursed." Nicodemus, one of their members who had come to him earlier, said to them, "Does our law condemn a man before it first hears him and finds out what he is doing?" They answered and said to him, "You are not from Galilee also, are you? Look and see that no prophet arises from Galilee."

Then each went to his own house.

Friends, today's Gospel reports the mixed reactions of people to Jesus' message. What does he say as he preaches? "Repent, for the kingdom of heaven is at hand!" We mustn't flatten this out or render it too spiritually abstract, as though he were talking only about becoming nicer people, more generous and more kind. His preaching was about more than that. It was part and parcel of his messianic vocation.

What he was saying was something like this: a new order is breaking out in Israel; the tribes are coming back together and Yahweh is going to reign. Therefore, adjust your lives, your vision, your expectations. Start living even now as members of this new kingdom.

The Israelites knew that a major task of the Messiah was to engage the enemies of Israel, to deal definitively with those powers opposed to God's creative purpose. This very much included political oppressors, religious charlatans, and self-absorbed Pharisees—all of whom Jesus deals with and confronts.

Reflect: All the baptized are grafted on to Christ, becoming Christified and acting in Christ's person. Our job description is thus the same as his. Are you working to gather the tribes into the new Israel, which is the Church? Are you actively taking on the enemies of the Lord?

MARCH 22, 2026

Fifth Sunday of Lent

John 11:1–45 (or 11:3–7, 17, 20–27, 33b–45)

Now a man was ill, Lazarus from Bethany, the village of Mary and her sister Martha. Mary was the one who had anointed the Lord with perfumed oil and dried his feet with her hair; it was her brother Lazarus who was ill. So the sisters sent word to him saying, "Master, the one you love is ill." When Jesus heard this he said, "This illness is not to end in death, but is for the glory of God, that the Son of God may be glorified through it." Now Jesus loved Martha and her sister and Lazarus. So when he heard that he was ill, he remained for two days in the place where he was. Then after this he said to his disciples, "Let us go back to Judea." The disciples said to him, "Rabbi, the Jews were just trying to stone you, and you want to go back there?" Jesus answered, "Are there not twelve hours in a day? If one walks during the day, he does not stumble, because he sees the light of this world. But if one walks at night, he stumbles, because the light is not in him." He said this, and then told them, "Our friend Lazarus is asleep, but I am going to awaken him." So the disciples said to him, "Master, if he is asleep, he will be saved." But Jesus was talking about his death, while they thought that he meant ordinary sleep. So then Jesus said to them clearly, "Lazarus has died. And I am glad for you that I was not there, that you may believe. Let us go to him." So Thomas, called Didymus, said to his fellow disciples, "Let us also go to die with him."

When Jesus arrived, he found that Lazarus had already been in the tomb for four days. Now Bethany was near Jerusalem, only about two miles away. And many of the Jews had come to Martha and Mary to comfort them about their brother. When Martha heard that Jesus was coming, she went to meet him; but Mary sat at home. Martha said to Jesus, "Lord, if you had been here, my brother would not have died. But even now I know that whatever you ask of God, God will give you." Jesus said to her, "Your brother will rise." Martha said to him, "I know he will rise, in the resurrection on the last day." Jesus told her, "I am the resurrection and the life; whoever believes in me, even if he dies, will live, and everyone who lives and believes in me will never die. Do you believe this?" She said to him, "Yes, Lord. I have come to believe that you are the Christ, the Son of God, the one who is coming into the world."

When she had said this, she went and called her sister Mary secretly, saying, "The teacher is here and is asking for you." As soon as she heard this, she rose quickly and went to him. For Jesus had not yet come into the village, but was still where Martha had met him. So when the Jews who were with her in the house comforting her saw Mary get up quickly and go out, they followed her, presuming that she was going to the tomb to weep there. When Mary came to where Jesus was and saw him, she fell at his feet and said to him, "Lord, if you had been here, my brother would not have died." When Jesus saw her weeping and the Jews who had come with her weeping, he became perturbed and deeply troubled, and said, "Where have you laid him?" They said to him, "Sir, come and see." And Jesus wept. So the Jews said, "See how he loved him." But some of them said, "Could not the one who opened the eyes of the blind man have done something so that this man would not have died?"

So Jesus, perturbed again, came to the tomb. It was a cave, and a stone lay across it. Jesus said, "Take away the stone." Martha, the dead man's sister, said to him, "Lord, by now there will be a stench; he has been dead for four days." Jesus said to her, "Did I not tell you that if you believe you will see the glory of God?" So they took away the stone. And Jesus raised his eyes and said, "Father, I thank you for hearing me. I know that you always hear me; but because of the crowd here I have said this, that they may believe that you sent me." And when he had said this, he cried out in a loud voice, "Lazarus, come out!" The dead man came out, tied hand and foot with burial bands, and his face was wrapped in a cloth. So Jesus said to them, "Untie him and let him go."

Now many of the Jews who had come to Mary and seen what he had done began to believe in him.

Friends, today's Gospel speaks of Jesus' conquest of death in the raising of Lazarus. What if death is not at all what God intended? Mind you, I mean death as we experience it—as something fearful, horrible, terrifying. This comes from having turned from God.

Jesus came primarily as a warrior whose final enemy is death. It is easy to domesticate Jesus, presenting him as a kindly moral teacher. But that is not how the Gospels present him. He is a cosmic warrior who has come to do battle with those forces that keep us from being fully alive.

Throughout the Gospels, Jesus deals with the effects of death and a death-obsessed culture: violence, hatred, egotism, exclusion, false religion, phony community. But the final enemy he must face down is death itself. Like Frodo going into Mordor, he has to go into death's domain, get into close quarters with it, and take it on.

Coming to Lazarus' tomb, Jesus feels the deepest emotions and begins to weep. This is God entering into the darkness, confusion, and agony of the death of sinners. He doesn't blithely stand above our situation, but rather takes it on and feels it at its deepest level.

Reflect: Meditate on how sin—the terrible clinging to self and attacking of others—flows finally from a fear of death, and on how Christ offers you freedom from thralldom to its ways.

MARCH 23, 2026

Monday of the Fifth Week of Lent

John 8:1–11

Jesus went to the Mount of Olives. But early in the morning he arrived again in the temple area, and all the people started coming to him, and he sat down and taught them. Then the scribes and the Pharisees brought a woman who had been caught in adultery and made her stand in the middle. They said to him, "Teacher, this woman was caught in the very act of committing adultery. Now in the law, Moses commanded us to stone such women. So what do you say?" They said this to test him, so that they could have some charge to bring against him. Jesus bent down and began to write on the ground with his finger. But when they continued asking him, he straightened up and said to them, "Let the one among you who is without sin be the first to throw a stone at her." Again he bent down and wrote on the ground. And in response, they went away one by one, beginning with the elders. So he was left alone with the woman before him. Then Jesus straightened up and said to her, "Woman, where are they? Has no one condemned you?" She replied, "No one, sir." Then Jesus said, "Neither do I condemn you. Go, and from now on do not sin any more."

Friends, our Gospel today tells about the woman that the scribes and Pharisees caught in adultery. Imagine where they were standing when they caught her in the very act. The voyeurism and perversion of these men! Then they come *en masse*, in the terrible enthusiasm of a mob, and they present the case to Jesus.

Now, what does Jesus do in the face of this violent mob? First, he writes on the ground. The mysterious writing might indicate the listing of the sins of each person in the group. As he said in another Gospel, "Remove the wooden beam from your eye first; then you will see clearly to remove the splinter from your brother's eye."

And then he says, "Let the one among you who is without sin be the first to throw a stone at her." He forces them to turn their accusing glance inward, where it belongs. Instead of projecting their violence outward on a scapegoat, they should honestly name and confront the dysfunction within themselves.

This story, like all the stories in the Gospels, is a foreshadowing of the great story toward which we are tending. Jesus will be put to death by a mob bent on scapegoating violence.

Reflect: When have you seen a community—of a false, ersatz variety—forming around the common hatred of a scapegoat? How can you follow Christ in refusing to cooperate with the blind psychology of the mob?

MARCH 24, 2026

Tuesday of the Fifth Week of Lent

John 8:21–30

Jesus said to the Pharisees: "I am going away and you will look for me, but you will die in your sin. Where I am going you cannot come." So the Jews said, "He is not going to kill himself, is he, because he said, 'Where I am going you cannot come'?" He said to them, "You belong to what is below, I belong to what is above. You belong to this world, but I do not belong to this world. That is why I told you that you will die in your sins. For if you do not believe that I AM, you will die in your sins." So they said to him, "Who are you?" Jesus said to them, "What I told you from the beginning. I have much to say about you in condemnation. But the one who sent me is true, and what I heard from him I tell the world." They did not realize that he was speaking to them of the Father. So Jesus said to them, "When you lift up the Son of Man, then you will realize that I AM, and that I do nothing on my own, but I say only what the Father taught me. The one who sent me is with me. He has not left me alone, because I always do what is pleasing to him." Because he spoke this way, many came to believe in him.

Friends, in today's Gospel, Jesus prophesies his Crucifixion and his Father's role in his coming death. What enabled the first Christians to hold up the cross, to sing its praises, to wear it as a decoration is the fact that God raised up and ratified precisely this crucified Jesus: "You killed him, but God raised him up." Therefore, God was involved in this terrible thing; God was there, working out his salvific purposes.

But what does this mean? There have been numerous attempts throughout the Christian centuries to name the salvific nature of the cross. Let me offer just one take on it. It became clear to the first Christians that somehow, on that terrible cross, sin had been dealt with. The curse of sin had been removed, taken care of. On that terrible cross, Jesus functioned as the "Lamb of God," sacrificed for sin.

Does this mean God the Father is a cruel taskmaster, demanding a bloody sacrifice so that his anger might be appeased? No. Jesus' Crucifixion was the opening up of the divine heart so that we could see that no sin of ours could finally separate us from the love of God.

Reflect: We killed God, and God came back in forgiving love. Therefore, every and any sin of ours is swallowed up in the divine compassion. Do you believe this?

MARCH 25, 2026

Solemnity of the Annunciation of the Lord

Luke 1:26–38

The angel Gabriel was sent from God to a town of Galilee called Nazareth, to a virgin betrothed to a man named Joseph, of the house of David, and the virgin's name was Mary. And coming to her, he said, "Hail, full of grace! The Lord is with you." But she was greatly troubled at what was said and pondered what sort of greeting this might be. Then the angel said to her, "Do not be afraid, Mary, for you have found favor with God. Behold, you will conceive in your womb and bear a son, and you shall name him Jesus. He will be great and will be called Son of the Most High, and the Lord God will give him the throne of David his father, and he will rule over the house of Jacob forever, and of his Kingdom there will be no end." But Mary said to the angel, "How can this be, since I have no relations with a man?" And the angel said to her in reply, "The Holy Spirit will come upon you, and the power of the Most High will overshadow you. Therefore the child to be born will be called holy, the Son of God. And behold, Elizabeth, your relative, has also conceived a son in her old age, and this is the sixth month for her who was called barren; for nothing will be impossible for God." Mary said, "Behold, I am the handmaid of the Lord. May it be done to me according to your word." Then the angel departed from her.

Friends, in today's Gospel, the angel Gabriel reveals to Mary that she will bear a son who will reign from David's throne.

As background, note that God had promised that David's throne would last forever, but his line had apparently been broken in 587 BC. Six hundred years later Gabriel appeared to Mary, who was betrothed to a man named Joseph of the house of David.

Greeting her as "full of grace," the angel announced that she will conceive in her womb and bear a son: "He will be great and will be called Son of the Most High." Then comes the kicker that would have taken the breath away from any first-century Jew listening to the story: "And the Lord God will give him the throne of David his father, and he will rule over the house of Jacob forever, and of his Kingdom there will be no end."

What seemed to have come to an end had in fact just gone underground, and was now ready to appear fully in the light. The kingly line of David was in fact unsevered, and now the full meaning of God's promise would be revealed.

Reflect: Have you ever been tempted to despair, to say that there is no rhyme or reason to things and that God is not in charge? Looking back, do you now appreciate the complexity and mystery of God's design?

MARCH 26, 2026

Thursday of the Fifth Week of Lent

John 8:51–59

Jesus said to the Jews: "Amen, amen, I say to you, whoever keeps my word will never see death." So the Jews said to him, "Now we are sure that you are possessed. Abraham died, as did the prophets, yet you say, 'Whoever keeps my word will never taste death.' Are you greater than our father Abraham, who died? Or the prophets, who died? Who do you make yourself out to be?" Jesus answered, "If I glorify myself, my glory is worth nothing; but it is my Father who glorifies me, of whom you say, 'He is our God.' You do not know him, but I know him. And if I should say that I do not know him, I would be like you a liar. But I do know him and I keep his word. Abraham your father rejoiced to see my day; he saw it and was glad." So the Jews said to him, "You are not yet fifty years old and you have seen Abraham?" Jesus said to them, "Amen, amen, I say to you, before Abraham came to be, I AM." So they picked up stones to throw at him; but Jesus hid and went out of the temple area.

Friends, today, Jesus refers to himself as "I AM," the name God revealed to Moses. So let's reflect on this episode from Exodus.

While tending sheep in the hill country, Moses sees a strange sight. There an angel of the Lord appears to him in fire, flaming out of a bush. God sees him and calls him by name: "Moses! Moses! . . . I am the God of your father, the God of Abraham, the God of Isaac, and the God of Jacob." This is a very familiar God, one who knows Moses' ancestors.

Moses makes bold to ask, "If I go to the Israelites and say to them, 'The God of your ancestors has sent me to you,' and they ask me, 'What is his name?' what do I tell them?" God replies: "I am who I am." What does that mean? God is saying, in essence, "I cannot be defined, described, or delimited. I am not a being, but rather the sheer act of *to-be* itself."

"This is what you will tell the Israelites: I AM has sent me to you." The sheer act of being itself cannot be avoided, and it cannot be controlled. It can only be surrendered to in faith. How shocking and strange Jesus' listeners must have found it when Jesus took this name for himself!

Reflect: When the God of the burning bush comes close to creatures, they are not consumed; rather, they become more beautifully and radiantly themselves—on fire but not burned up. Where do you see this spiritual dynamic at work in the Church? How has closeness to God made you more fully alive?

MARCH 27, 2026

Friday of the Fifth Week of Lent

John 10:31–42

The Jews picked up rocks to stone Jesus. Jesus answered them, "I have shown you many good works from my Father. For which of these are you trying to stone me?" The Jews answered him, "We are not stoning you for a good work but for blasphemy. You, a man, are making yourself God." Jesus answered them, "Is it not written in your law, 'I said, "You are gods"'? If it calls them gods to whom the word of God came, and Scripture cannot be set aside, can you say that the one whom the Father has consecrated and sent into the world blasphemes because I said, 'I am the Son of God'? If I do not perform my Father's works, do not believe me; but if I perform them, even if you do not believe me, believe the works, so that you may realize and understand that the Father is in me and I am in the Father." Then they tried again to arrest him; but he escaped from their power.

He went back across the Jordan to the place where John first baptized, and there he remained. Many came to him and said, "John performed no sign, but everything John said about this man was true." And many there began to believe in him.

Friends, in today's Gospel, Jewish leaders attempt to stone Jesus because he claimed to be the Son of God. He defends his identity, saying, "If I do not perform my Father's works, do not believe me; but if I perform them, even if you do not believe me, believe the works, so that you may realize and understand that the Father is in me and I am in the Father."

At the Last Supper, Jesus would further explain his intimate relationship with the Father. There he lays out for us the coinherence that obtains at the most fundamental dimension of being—that is to say, within the very existence of God. "Master," Philip said to him, "Show us the Father, and that will be enough for us." Jesus replied, "Have I been with you for so long a time and you still do not know me, Philip? Whoever has seen me has seen the Father."

How can this be true, unless the Father and the Son coinhere in each other? Though Father and Son are truly distinct, they are utterly implicated in each other by a mutual act of love. As Jesus says, "The Father who dwells in me is doing his works."

Reflect: If you want access to the divine coinherence, you must walk the path of love laid out by Jesus. To what degree do you follow Christ's ethic of radical love, even the love of enemies? In what ways do you still oppose the divine way of being through jealousy, hatred, violence, racism, or clinging to your privileges?

MARCH 28, 2026

Saturday of the Fifth Week of Lent

John 11:45–56

Many of the Jews who had come to Mary and seen what Jesus had done began to believe in him. But some of them went to the Pharisees and told them what Jesus had done. So the chief priests and the Pharisees convened the Sanhedrin and said, "What are we going to do? This man is performing many signs. If we leave him alone, all will believe in him, and the Romans will come and take away both our land and our nation." But one of them, Caiaphas, who was high priest that year, said to them, "You know nothing, nor do you consider that it is better for you that one man should die instead of the people, so that the whole nation may not perish." He did not say this on his own, but since he was high priest for that year, he prophesied that Jesus was going to die for the nation, and not only for the nation, but also to gather into one the dispersed children of God. So from that day on they planned to kill him.

So Jesus no longer walked about in public among the Jews, but he left for the region near the desert, to a town called Ephraim, and there he remained with his disciples.

Now the Passover of the Jews was near, and many went up from the country to Jerusalem before Passover to purify themselves. They looked for Jesus and said to one another as they were in the temple area, "What do you think? That he will not come to the feast?"

Friends, in today's Gospel, the chief priests and Pharisees unite in a plot to kill Jesus because he raised Lazarus from the dead.

The Crucifixion of Jesus is a classic instance of Catholic philosopher René Girard's scapegoating theory. He held that a society, large or small, that finds itself in conflict comes together through a common act of blaming an individual or group purportedly responsible for the conflict.

It is utterly consistent with the Girardian theory that Caiaphas, the leading religious figure of the time, says to his colleagues, "It is better for you that one man should die instead of the people, so that the whole nation may not perish."

In any other religious context, this sort of rationalization would be validated. But in the Resurrection of Jesus from the dead, this stunning truth is revealed: God is not on the side of the scapegoaters, but rather on the side of the scapegoated victim.

The true God does not sanction a community created through violence; rather, he sanctions what Jesus called the kingdom of God, a society grounded in forgiveness, love, and identification with the victim.

Reflect: Where do you find this unveiling of the scapegoating mechanism in the Gospels and in Christian literature?

MARCH 29, 2026

Palm Sunday of the Passion of the Lord

Matthew 26:14—27:66 (or 27:11–54)

One of the Twelve, who was called Judas Iscariot, went to the chief priests and said, "What are you willing to give me if I hand him over to you?" They paid him thirty pieces of silver, and from that time on he looked for an opportunity to hand him over.

On the first day of the Feast of Unleavened Bread, the disciples approached Jesus and said, "Where do you want us to prepare for you to eat the Passover?" He said, "Go into the city to a certain man and tell him, 'The teacher says, "My appointed time draws near; in your house I shall celebrate the Passover with my disciples."'" The disciples then did as Jesus had ordered, and prepared the Passover.

When it was evening, he reclined at table with the Twelve. And while they were eating, he said, "Amen, I say to you, one of you will betray me." Deeply distressed at this, they began to say to him one after another, "Surely it is not I, Lord?" He said in reply, "He who has dipped his hand into the dish with me is the one who will betray me. The Son of Man indeed goes, as it is written of him, but woe to that man by whom the Son of Man is betrayed. It would be better for that man if he had never been born." Then Judas, his betrayer, said in reply, "Surely it is not I, Rabbi?" He answered, "You have said so."

While they were eating, Jesus took bread, said the blessing, broke it, and giving it to his disciples said, "Take and eat; this is my body." Then he took a cup, gave thanks, and gave it to them, saying, "Drink from it, all of you, for this is my blood of the covenant, which will be shed on behalf of many for the forgiveness of sins. I tell you, from now on I shall not drink this fruit of the vine until the day when I drink it with you new in the kingdom of my Father." Then, after singing a hymn, they went out to the Mount of Olives.

Then Jesus said to them, "This night all of you will have your faith in me shaken, for it is written:

I will strike the shepherd,
and the sheep of the flock will be dispersed;

but after I have been raised up, I shall go before you to Galilee." Peter said to him in reply, "Though all may have their faith in you shaken, mine will never be." Jesus said to him, "Amen, I say to you, this very night before the cock crows, you will deny me three times." Peter said to him, "Even though I should have to die with you, I will not deny you." And all the disciples spoke likewise.

Then Jesus came with them to a place called Gethsemane, and he said to his disciples, "Sit here while I go over there and pray." He took along Peter and the two sons of Zebedee, and began to feel sorrow and distress. Then he said to them, "My soul is sorrowful even to death. Remain here and keep watch with me." He advanced a little and fell prostrate in prayer, saying, "My Father, if it is possible, let this cup pass from me; yet, not as I will, but as you will." When he returned to his disciples he found them asleep. He said to Peter, "So you could not keep watch with me for one hour? Watch and pray that you may not undergo the test. The spirit is willing, but the flesh is weak." Withdrawing a second time, he prayed again, "My Father, if it is not possible that this cup pass without my drinking it, your will be done!" Then he returned once more and found them asleep, for they could not keep their eyes open. He left them and withdrew again and prayed a third time, saying the same thing again. Then he returned to his disciples and said to them,

"Are you still sleeping and taking your rest? Behold, the hour is at hand when the Son of Man is to be handed over to sinners. Get up, let us go. Look, my betrayer is at hand."

While he was still speaking, Judas, one of the Twelve, arrived, accompanied by a large crowd, with swords and clubs, who had come from the chief priests and the elders of the people. His betrayer had arranged a sign with them, saying, "The man I shall kiss is the one; arrest him." Immediately he went over to Jesus and said, "Hail, Rabbi!" and he kissed him. Jesus answered him, "Friend, do what you have come for." Then stepping forward they laid hands on Jesus and arrested him. And behold, one of those who accompanied Jesus put his hand to his sword, drew it, and struck the high priest's servant, cutting off his ear. Then Jesus said to him, "Put your sword back into its sheath, for all who take the sword will perish by the sword. Do you think that I cannot call upon my Father and he will not provide me at this moment with more than twelve legions of angels? But then how would the Scriptures be fulfilled which say that it must come to pass in this way?" At that hour Jesus said to the crowds, "Have you come out as against a robber, with swords and clubs to seize me? Day after day I sat teaching in the temple area, yet you did not arrest me. But all this has come to pass that the writings of the prophets may be fulfilled." Then all the disciples left him and fled.

Those who had arrested Jesus led him away to Caiaphas the high priest, where the scribes and the elders were assembled. Peter was following him at a distance as far as the high priest's courtyard, and going inside he sat down with the servants to see the outcome. The chief priests and the entire Sanhedrin kept trying to obtain false testimony against Jesus in order to put him to death, but they found none, though many false witnesses came forward. Finally two came forward who stated, "This man said, 'I can destroy the temple of God and within three days rebuild it.'" The high priest rose and addressed him, "Have you no answer? What are these men testifying against you?" But Jesus was silent. Then the high priest said to him, "I order you to tell us under oath before the living God whether you are the Christ, the Son of God." Jesus said to him in reply, "You have said so. But I tell you:

From now on you will see 'the Son of Man
seated at the right hand of the Power'
and 'coming on the clouds of heaven.'"

Then the high priest tore his robes and said, "He has blasphemed! What further need have we of witnesses? You have now heard the blasphemy; what is your opinion?" They said in reply, "He deserves to die!" Then they spat in his face and struck him, while some slapped him, saying, "Prophesy for us, Christ: who is it that struck you?"

Now Peter was sitting outside in the courtyard. One of the maids came over to him and said, "You too were with Jesus the Galilean." But he denied it in front of everyone, saying, "I do not know what you are talking about!" As he went out to the gate, another girl saw him and said to those who were there, "This man was with Jesus the Nazorean." Again he denied it with an oath, "I do not know the man!" A little later the bystanders came over and said to Peter, "Surely you too are one of them; even your speech gives you away." At that he began to curse and to swear, "I do not know the man." And immediately a cock crowed. Then Peter remembered the word that Jesus had spoken: "Before the cock crows you will deny me three times." He went out and began to weep bitterly.

When it was morning, all the chief priests and the elders of the people took counsel against Jesus to put him to death. They bound him, led him away, and handed him over to Pilate, the governor.

Then Judas, his betrayer, seeing that Jesus had been condemned, deeply regretted what he had done. He returned the thirty pieces of silver to the chief priests and elders, saying, "I have sinned in betraying innocent blood." They said, "What is that to us? Look to it yourself." Flinging the money into the temple, he departed and went off and hanged himself. The chief priests gathered up the money, but said, "It is not lawful to deposit this in the temple treasury, for it is the price of blood." After consultation, they used it to buy the potter's field as a burial place for foreigners. That is why that field even today is called the Field of Blood. Then was fulfilled what had been said through Jeremiah the prophet, *And they took the thirty pieces of silver, the value of a man with a price on his head, a price set by some of the Israelites, and they paid it out for the potter's field just as the Lord had commanded me.*

Now Jesus stood before the governor, and he questioned him, "Are you the king of the Jews?" Jesus said, "You say so." And when he was accused by the chief priests and elders, he made no answer.

Then Pilate said to him, "Do you not hear how many things they are testifying against you?" But he did not answer him one word, so that the governor was greatly amazed.

Now on the occasion of the feast the governor was accustomed to release to the crowd one prisoner whom they wished. And at that time they had a notorious prisoner called Barabbas. So when they had assembled, Pilate said to them, "Which one do you want me to release to you, Barabbas, or Jesus called Christ?" For he knew that it was out of envy that they had handed him over. While he was still seated on the bench, his wife sent him a message, "Have nothing to do with that righteous man. I suffered much in a dream today because of him." The chief priests and the elders persuaded the crowds to ask for Barabbas but to destroy Jesus. The governor said to them in reply, "Which of the two do you want me to release to you?" They answered, "Barabbas!" Pilate said to them, "Then what shall I do with Jesus called Christ?" They all said, "Let him be crucified!" But he said, "Why? What evil has he done?" They only shouted the louder, "Let him be crucified!" When Pilate saw that he was not succeeding at all, but that a riot was breaking out instead, he took water and washed his hands in the sight of the crowd, saying, "I am innocent of this man's blood. Look to it yourselves." And the whole people said in reply, "His blood be upon us and upon our children." Then he released Barabbas to them, but after he had Jesus scourged, he handed him over to be crucified.

Then the soldiers of the governor took Jesus inside the praetorium and gathered the whole cohort around him. They stripped off his clothes and threw a scarlet military cloak about him. Weaving a crown out of thorns, they placed it on his head, and a reed in his right hand. And kneeling before him, they mocked him, saying, "Hail, King of the Jews!" They spat upon him and took the reed and kept striking him on the head. And when they had mocked him, they stripped him of the cloak, dressed him in his own clothes, and led him off to crucify him.

As they were going out, they met a Cyrenian named Simon; this man they pressed into service to carry his cross.

And when they came to a place called Golgotha—which means Place of the Skull—, they gave Jesus wine to drink mixed with gall. But when he had tasted it, he refused to drink. After they had crucified him, they divided his garments by casting lots; then they sat down and kept watch over him there. And they placed over his head the written charge against him: This is Jesus, the King of the Jews. Two revolutionaries were crucified with him, one on his right and the other on his left. Those passing by reviled him, shaking their heads and saying, "You who would destroy the temple and rebuild it in three days, save yourself, if you are the Son of God, and come down from the cross!" Likewise the chief priests with the scribes and elders mocked him and said, "He saved others; he cannot save himself. So he is the king of Israel! Let him come down from the cross now, and we will believe in him. He trusted in God; let him deliver him now if he wants him. For he said, 'I am the Son of God.'" The revolutionaries who were crucified with him also kept abusing him in the same way.

From noon onward, darkness came over the whole land until three in the afternoon. And about three o'clock Jesus cried out in a loud voice, *"Eli, Eli, lema sabachthani?"* which means, "My God, my God, why have you forsaken me?" Some of the bystanders who heard it said, "This one is calling for Elijah." Immediately one of them ran to get a sponge; he soaked it in wine, and putting it on a reed, gave it to him to drink. But the rest said, "Wait, let us see if Elijah comes to save him." But Jesus cried out again in a loud voice, and gave up his spirit.

Here all kneel and pause for a short time.

And behold, the veil of the sanctuary was torn in two from top to bottom. The earth quaked, rocks were split, tombs were opened, and the bodies of many saints who had fallen asleep were raised. And coming forth from their tombs after his resurrection, they entered the holy city and appeared to many. The centurion and the men with him who were keeping watch over Jesus feared greatly when they saw the earthquake and all that was happening, and they said, "Truly, this was the Son of God!" There were many women there, looking on from a distance, who had followed Jesus from Galilee, ministering to him. Among them were Mary Magdalene and Mary the mother of James and Joseph, and the mother of the sons of Zebedee.

When it was evening, there came a rich man from Arimathea named Joseph, who was himself a disciple of Jesus. He went to Pilate and asked for the body of Jesus; then Pilate ordered it to be handed over. Taking the body, Joseph wrapped it in clean linen and laid it in his new tomb that he had hewn in the rock. Then he rolled a huge stone across the entrance to the tomb and departed. But Mary Magdalene and the other Mary remained sitting there, facing the tomb.

The next day, the one following the day of preparation, the chief priests and the Pharisees gathered before Pilate and said, "Sir, we remember that this impostor while still alive said, 'After three days I will be raised up.' Give orders, then, that the grave be secured until the third day, lest his disciples come and steal him and say to the people, 'He has been raised from the dead.' This last imposture would be worse than the first." Pilate said to them, "The guard is yours; go, secure it as best you can." So they went and secured the tomb by fixing a seal to the stone and setting the guard.

Friends, on this Palm Sunday, Matthew's magnificent Gospel of the Passion bids us to reflect on the seriousness of sin.

To be sure, the Gospel proclaimed by the first Christians involves the glorious Resurrection, but those initial evangelists never let their hearers forget that the one who had been raised was none other than the one who had been crucified.

So the question was—and remains—why would God's salvation of the human race have to include something as horrifying as the Crucifixion of the Son of God?

Here's the point. The scriptural authors understand sin not so much as a series of acts as a condition in which we are stuck. No amount of merely human effort could possibly solve the problem. Something awful had to be done on our behalf in order to offset the awfulness of sin.

With this biblical realism in mind, we can begin to comprehend why the Crucifixion of the Son of God was necessary. The just rapport between God and human beings could not be reestablished either through our moral effort or with simply a word of forgiveness. Something had to be *done*—and God alone could do it.

Reflect: Meditate today on the sheer strangeness of the Crucifixion and the weight of sin.

MARCH 30, 2026

Monday of Holy Week

John 12:1–11

Six days before Passover Jesus came to Bethany, where Lazarus was, whom Jesus had raised from the dead. They gave a dinner for him there, and Martha served, while Lazarus was one of those reclining at table with him. Mary took a liter of costly perfumed oil made from genuine aromatic nard and anointed the feet of Jesus and dried them with her hair; the house was filled with the fragrance of the oil. Then Judas the Iscariot, one of his disciples, and the one who would betray him, said, "Why was this oil not sold for three hundred days' wages and given to the poor?" He said this not because he cared about the poor but because he was a thief and held the money bag and used to steal the contributions. So Jesus said, "Leave her alone. Let her keep this for the day of my burial. You always have the poor with you, but you do not always have me."

The large crowd of the Jews found out that he was there and came, not only because of him, but also to see Lazarus, whom he had raised from the dead. And the chief priests plotted to kill Lazarus too, because many of the Jews were turning away and believing in Jesus because of him.

Friends, in today's Gospel, Mary of Bethany anoints Jesus for his death and burial. By this act, she anticipates the visit of three women to the tomb of Jesus. Early on the morning of the first day of the week, Mary Magdalene, Mary the mother of James, and Salome will bring spices to anoint the body of Jesus.

They will look in and see a young man—and be frightened out of their wits. Can you imagine? You walk into a tomb, fully expecting to see a dead body, and you see instead someone alive and well—someone different than the man who was buried there! But that will not be the end of their surprise. The man will announce that the Jesus whom they seek is not there, that he has been raised up and will go ahead of them into Galilee.

From this grave of Jesus we will learn that everything we took to be the case is not the case. God is the enemy of death, and he has shown us his power over death in the most unambiguous way. Our lives no longer need to be dominated by the fear of death, and we see the proof of this in the most vivid way imaginable.

Keep all of that in mind as we read this beautiful story of Mary of Bethany anointing the feet of Jesus.

Reflect: Some people think that they will make the Resurrection more intelligible, more acceptable to modern people, if they allegorize it away, turning it into a vague symbol of the perdurance of Jesus' cause. How would you respond to this?

MARCH 31, 2026

Tuesday of Holy Week

John 13:21–33, 36–38

Reclining at table with his disciples, Jesus was deeply troubled and testified, "Amen, amen, I say to you, one of you will betray me." The disciples looked at one another, at a loss as to whom he meant. One of his disciples, the one whom Jesus loved, was reclining at Jesus' side. So Simon Peter nodded to him to find out whom he meant. He leaned back against Jesus' chest and said to him, "Master, who is it?" Jesus answered, "It is the one to whom I hand the morsel after I have dipped it." So he dipped the morsel and took it and handed it to Judas, son of Simon the Iscariot. After Judas took the morsel, Satan entered him. So Jesus said to him, "What you are going to do, do quickly." Now none of those reclining at table realized why he said this to him. Some thought that since Judas kept the money bag, Jesus had told him, "Buy what we need for the feast," or to give something to the poor. So Judas took the morsel and left at once. And it was night.

When he had left, Jesus said, "Now is the Son of Man glorified, and God is glorified in him. If God is glorified in him, God will also glorify him in himself, and he will glorify him at once. My children, I will be with you only a little while longer. You will look for me, and as I told the Jews, 'Where I go you cannot come,' so now I say it to you."

Simon Peter said to him, "Master, where are you going?" Jesus answered him, "Where I am going, you cannot follow me now, though you will follow later." Peter said to him, "Master, why can I not follow you now? I will lay down my life for you." Jesus answered, "Will you lay down your life for me? Amen, amen, I say to you, the cock will not crow before you deny me three times."

Friends, in today's Gospel, Jesus foretells the denial of Peter, which is fulfilled in the account of the Passion. Peter later denies Jesus three times before the cock crows and, remembering Jesus' prediction, breaks down and weeps.

After the Resurrection, Peter and the other disciples returned to Galilee to work as fishermen again, and there spotted Jesus on the far shore. As Jesus draws Peter back into his circle of intimacy, we witness a beautiful act of spiritual direction. Three times the Lord asks Peter whether he loves him, and three times Peter affirms it: "Lord, you know that I love you."

St. Augustine was the first to comment that the threefold statement of love was meant to counteract the threefold denial. Peter emerges as the archetype of the forgiven and commissioned Church, for after each of his reaffirmations, Peter hears the command to tend the sheep. Once we are brought back into friendship with Jesus, we are called to love those whom he loves.

Reflect: Christianity is not a set of ideas or convictions or principles. It is a relationship with a person. Do you love Jesus? Has he become your friend?

APRIL 1, 2026

Wednesday of Holy Week

Matthew 26:14–25

One of the Twelve, who was called Judas Iscariot, went to the chief priests and said, "What are you willing to give me if I hand him over to you?" They paid him thirty pieces of silver, and from that time on he looked for an opportunity to hand him over.

On the first day of the Feast of Unleavened Bread, the disciples approached Jesus and said, "Where do you want us to prepare for you to eat the Passover?" He said, "Go into the city to a certain man and tell him, 'The teacher says, "My appointed time draws near; in your house I shall celebrate the Passover with my disciples."'" The disciples then did as Jesus had ordered, and prepared the Passover.

When it was evening, he reclined at table with the Twelve. And while they were eating, he said, "Amen, I say to you, one of you will betray me." Deeply distressed at this, they began to say to him one after another, "Surely it is not I, Lord?" He said in reply, "He who has dipped his hand into the dish with me is the one who will betray me. The Son of Man indeed goes, as it is written of him, but woe to that man by whom the Son of Man is betrayed. It would be better for that man if he had never been born." Then Judas, his betrayer, said in reply, "Surely it is not I, Rabbi?" He answered, "You have said so."

Friends, today's Gospel is from Matthew's account of the Last Supper, where Jesus acknowledges Judas as his betrayer.

God's desires have been, from the beginning, opposed. Consistently, human beings have preferred the isolation of sin to the festivity of the sacred meal. Theologians have called this anomalous tendency the *mysterium iniquitatis* (the mystery of iniquity), for there is no rational ground for it, no reason for it to exist.

But there it stubbornly is, always shadowing the good, parasitic upon that which it tries to destroy. Therefore, we should not be too surprised that, as the sacred meal comes to its richest possible expression, evil accompanies it.

Judas the betrayer expresses the *mysterium iniquitatis* with particular symbolic power, for he had spent years in intimacy with Jesus, taking in the Lord's moves and thoughts at close quarters, sharing the table of fellowship with him—and yet he saw fit to turn Jesus over to his enemies and to interrupt the coinherence of the Last Supper.

Those of us who regularly gather around the table of intimacy with Christ and yet engage consistently in the works of darkness are meant to see ourselves in the betrayer.

Reflect: The tradition speaks of God permitting certain evils so as to bring about a greater good. Where have you seen this principle verified? And why is the cross the only adequate "resolution," finally, to the problem of evil?

APRIL 2, 2026

Thursday of the Lord's Supper (Holy Thursday)

John 13:1–15

Before the feast of Passover, Jesus knew that his hour had come to pass from this world to the Father. He loved his own in the world and he loved them to the end. The devil had already induced Judas, son of Simon the Iscariot, to hand him over. So, during supper, fully aware that the Father had put everything into his power and that he had come from God and was returning to God, he rose from supper and took off his outer garments. He took a towel and tied it around his waist. Then he poured water into a basin and began to wash the disciples' feet and dry them with the towel around his waist. He came to Simon Peter, who said to him, "Master, are you going to wash my feet?" Jesus answered and said to him, "What I am doing, you do not understand now, but you will understand later." Peter said to him, "You will never wash my feet." Jesus answered him, "Unless I wash you, you will have no inheritance with me." Simon Peter said to him, "Master, then not only my feet, but my hands and head as well." Jesus said to him, "Whoever has bathed has no need except to have his feet washed, for he is clean all over; so you are clean, but not all." For he knew who would betray him; for this reason, he said, "Not all of you are clean."

So when he had washed their feet and put his garments back on and reclined at table again, he said to them, "Do you realize what I have done for you? You call me 'teacher' and 'master,' and rightly so, for indeed I am. If I, therefore, the master and teacher, have washed your feet, you ought to wash one another's feet. I have given you a model to follow, so that as I have done for you, you should also do."

Friends, in today's Gospel, Jesus gathers with his chosen twelve at the climax of his life and does something so strange that we still wonder at it two thousand years later: he takes off his outer garment, puts a towel around his waist, and begins to wash his disciples' feet.

The nineteenth-century philosopher Hegel said that all human society, to varying degrees, is characterized by the master-slave dynamic. Long before Hegel, the great St. Augustine noticed what he called the *libido dominandi*, the "lust to dominate," as the mark of a dysfunctional society. Long before Augustine, the authors of the Old Testament were also interested in this problem, because the central story of the Scriptures is that of slavery and liberation from slavery—the Passover event.

But we see now in John's Gospel how the distinctive mark of Jesus' kingdom is precisely the overturning of the master-slave dynamic. Jesus bends down to do the work that was so lowly and frankly gross that only the lowest of the slaves were expected to do it, and he says, "As I have done for you, you should also do." And what does he do later at the same supper? He gives himself away entirely in the Eucharist: "This is my body, which will be given for you."

It is into this new dynamic that we are invited by Jesus: the washing of the feet, the giving away of body and blood.

Reflect: What lowly work on behalf of God's kingdom might you do over the next three days, adopting the attitude of a servant—humble, simple, and forgotten?

APRIL 3, 2026

Friday of the Passion of the Lord (Good Friday)

John 18:1—19:42

Jesus went out with his disciples across the Kidron valley to where there was a garden, into which he and his disciples entered. Judas his betrayer also knew the place, because Jesus had often met there with his disciples. So Judas got a band of soldiers and guards from the chief priests and the Pharisees and went there with lanterns, torches, and weapons. Jesus, knowing everything that was going to happen to him, went out and said to them, "Whom are you looking for?" They answered him, "Jesus the Nazorean." He said to them, "I AM." Judas his betrayer was also with them. When he said to them, "I AM," they turned away and fell to the ground. So he again asked them, "Whom are you looking for?" They said, "Jesus the Nazorean." Jesus answered, "I told you that I AM. So if you are looking for me, let these men go." This was to fulfill what he had said, "I have not lost any of those you gave me." Then Simon Peter, who had a sword, drew it, struck the high priest's slave, and cut off his right ear. The slave's name was Malchus. Jesus said to Peter, "Put your sword into its scabbard. Shall I not drink the cup that the Father gave me?"

So the band of soldiers, the tribune, and the Jewish guards seized Jesus, bound him, and brought him to Annas first. He was the father-in-law of Caiaphas, who was high priest that year. It was Caiaphas who had counseled the Jews that it was better that one man should die rather than the people.

Simon Peter and another disciple followed Jesus. Now the other disciple was known to the high priest, and he entered the courtyard of the high priest with Jesus. But Peter stood at the gate outside. So the other disciple, the acquaintance of the high priest, went out and spoke to the gatekeeper and brought Peter in. Then the maid who was the gatekeeper said to Peter, "You are not one of this man's disciples, are you?" He said, "I am not." Now the slaves and the guards were standing around a charcoal fire that they had made, because it was cold, and were warming themselves. Peter was also standing there keeping warm.

The high priest questioned Jesus about his disciples and about his doctrine. Jesus answered him, "I have spoken publicly to the world. I have always taught in a synagogue or in the temple area where all the Jews gather, and in secret I have said nothing. Why ask me? Ask those who heard me what I said to them. They know what I said." When he had said this, one of the temple guards standing there struck Jesus and said, "Is this the way you answer the high priest?" Jesus answered him, "If I have spoken wrongly, testify to the wrong; but if I have spoken rightly, why do you strike me?" Then Annas sent him bound to Caiaphas the high priest.

Now Simon Peter was standing there keeping warm. And they said to him, "You are not one of his disciples, are you?" He denied it and said, "I am not." One of the slaves of the high priest, a relative of the one whose ear Peter had cut off, said, "Didn't I see you in the garden with him?" Again Peter denied it. And immediately the cock crowed.

Then they brought Jesus from Caiaphas to the praetorium. It was morning. And they themselves did not enter the praetorium, in order not to be defiled so that they could eat the Passover. So Pilate came out to them and said, "What charge do you bring against this man?" They answered and said to him, "If he were not a criminal, we would not have handed him over to you." At this, Pilate said to them, "Take him yourselves, and judge him according to your law." The Jews answered him, "We do not have the right to execute anyone," in order that the word of Jesus might be fulfilled that he said indicating the kind of death he would die. So Pilate went back into the praetorium and summoned Jesus and said to him, "Are you the King of the Jews?" Jesus answered, "Do you say this on your own or have others told you about me?" Pilate answered, "I am not a Jew, am I? Your own nation and the chief priests handed you over to me. What have you done?" Jesus answered, "My kingdom does not belong to this world. If my kingdom did belong to this world, my attendants would be fighting to keep me from being handed over to the Jews. But as it is, my kingdom is not here." So Pilate said to him, "Then you are a king?" Jesus answered, "You say I am a king. For this I was born and for this I came into the world, to testify to the truth. Everyone who belongs to the truth listens to my voice." Pilate said to him, "What is truth?"

When he had said this, he again went out to the Jews and said to them, "I find no guilt in him. But you have a custom that I release one prisoner to you at Passover. Do you want me to release to you the King of the Jews?" They cried out again, "Not this one but Barabbas!" Now Barabbas was a revolutionary.

Then Pilate took Jesus and had him scourged. And the soldiers wove a crown out of thorns and placed it on his head, and clothed him in a purple cloak, and they came to him and said, "Hail, King of the Jews!" And they struck him repeatedly. Once more Pilate went out and said to them, "Look, I am bringing him out to you, so that you may know that I find no guilt in him." So Jesus came out, wearing the crown of thorns and the purple cloak. And he said to them, "Behold, the man!" When the chief priests and the guards saw him they cried out, "Crucify him, crucify him!" Pilate said to them, "Take him yourselves and crucify him. I find no guilt in him." The Jews answered, "We have a law, and according to that law he ought to die, because he made himself the Son of God." Now when Pilate heard this statement, he became even more afraid, and went back into the praetorium and said to Jesus, "Where are you from?" Jesus did not answer him. So Pilate said to him, "Do you not speak to me? Do you not know that I have power to release you and I have power to crucify you?" Jesus answered him, "You would have no power over me if it had not been given to you from above. For this reason the one who handed me over to you has the greater sin." Consequently, Pilate tried to release him; but the Jews cried out, "If you release him, you are not a Friend of Caesar. Everyone who makes himself a king opposes Caesar."

When Pilate heard these words he brought Jesus out and seated him on the judge's bench in the place called Stone Pavement, in Hebrew, Gabbatha. It was preparation day for Passover, and it was about noon. And he said to the Jews, "Behold, your king!" They cried out, "Take him away, take him away! Crucify him!" Pilate said to them, "Shall I crucify your king?" The chief priests answered, "We have no king but Caesar." Then he handed him over to them to be crucified.

So they took Jesus, and, carrying the cross himself, he went out to what is called the Place of the Skull, in Hebrew, Golgotha. There they crucified him, and with him two others, one on either side, with Jesus in the middle. Pilate also had an inscription written and put on the cross. It read, "Jesus the Nazorean, the King of the Jews." Now many of the Jews read this inscription, because the place where Jesus was crucified was near the city; and it was written in Hebrew, Latin, and Greek. So the chief priests of the Jews said to Pilate, "Do not write 'The King of the Jews,' but that he said, 'I am the King of the Jews.'" Pilate answered, "What I have written, I have written."

When the soldiers had crucified Jesus, they took his clothes and divided them into four shares, a share for each soldier. They also took his tunic, but the tunic was seamless, woven in one piece from the top down. So they said to one another, "Let's not tear it, but cast lots for it to see whose it will be," in order that the passage of Scripture might be fulfilled that says:

They divided my garments among them,
and for my vesture they cast lots.

This is what the soldiers did. Standing by the cross of Jesus were his mother and his mother's sister, Mary the wife of Clopas, and Mary of Magdala. When Jesus saw his mother and the disciple there whom he loved he said to his mother, "Woman, behold, your son." Then he said to the disciple, "Behold, your mother." And from that hour the disciple took her into his home.

After this, aware that everything was now finished, in order that the Scripture might be fulfilled, Jesus said, "I thirst." There was a vessel filled with common wine. So they put a sponge soaked in wine on a sprig of hyssop and put it up to his mouth. When Jesus had taken the wine, he said, "It is finished." And bowing his head, he handed over the spirit.

Here all kneel and pause for a short time.

Now since it was preparation day, in order that the bodies might not remain on the cross on the sabbath, for the sabbath day of that week was a solemn one, the Jews asked Pilate that their legs be broken and that they be taken down. So the soldiers came and broke the legs of the first and then of the other one who was crucified with Jesus. But when they came to Jesus and saw that he was already dead, they did not break his legs, but one soldier thrust his lance into his side, and immediately blood and water flowed out. An eyewitness has testified, and his testimony is true; he knows that he is speaking the truth, so that you also may come to believe. For this happened so that the Scripture passage might be fulfilled:

Not a bone of it will be broken.
And again another passage says:
They will look upon him whom they have pierced.

After this, Joseph of Arimathea, secretly a disciple of Jesus for fear of the Jews, asked Pilate if he could remove the body of Jesus. And Pilate permitted it. So he came and took his body. Nicodemus, the one who had first come to him at night, also came bringing a mixture of myrrh and aloes weighing about one hundred pounds. They took the body of Jesus and bound it with burial cloths along with the spices, according to the Jewish burial custom. Now in the place where he had been crucified there was a garden, and in the garden a new tomb, in which no one had yet been buried. So they laid Jesus there because of the Jewish preparation day; for the tomb was close by.

Friends, our Gospel today is St. John's poignant account of the arrest of Jesus. The setting is the Garden of Gethsemane. Jesus has just been betrayed by Judas, seized, arrested, and bound; the ear of the high priest's slave has been severed; all of Jesus' disciples have fled.

In a parallel narrative, St. Mark adds this odd detail of the young man running off naked into the night. Like a Renaissance painter who puts contemporary figures into a biblical scene, here Mark places a stand-in for you and me in the scene. The young man is described as "following" Jesus. This, of course, is biblical code for discipleship.

And what is he wearing? The term used in the Greek (*sindona*) designates the kind of garment worn by the newly baptized. The point is this: to be a baptized member of Christ's Church is to put oneself in harm's way.

To be a follower of Jesus is to walk a dangerous path, one sure to upset the powers that be. The shame of this young man is that, at the moment of truth, he fled, leaving his precious baptismal garment in the hands of Jesus' enemies.

Reflect: What do you do at the moment of truth?

APRIL 4, 2026

Holy Saturday (Easter Vigil)

Matthew 28:1–10

After the sabbath, as the first day of the week was dawning, Mary Magdalene and the other Mary came to see the tomb. And behold, there was a great earthquake; for an angel of the Lord descended from heaven, approached, rolled back the stone, and sat upon it. His appearance was like lightning and his clothing was white as snow. The guards were shaken with fear of him and became like dead men. Then the angel said to the women in reply, "Do not be afraid! I know that you are seeking Jesus the crucified. He is not here, for he has been raised just as he said. Come and see the place where he lay. Then go quickly and tell his disciples, 'He has been raised from the dead, and he is going before you to Galilee; there you will see him.' Behold, I have told you." Then they went away quickly from the tomb, fearful yet overjoyed, and ran to announce this to his disciples. And behold, Jesus met them on their way and greeted them. They approached, embraced his feet, and did him homage. Then Jesus said to them, "Do not be afraid. Go tell my brothers to go to Galilee, and there they will see me."

Friends, on this Holy Saturday, in our Gospel we hear St. Matthew's account of the Resurrection. The Resurrection of Jesus from the dead is the be-all and end-all of the Christian faith. If Jesus didn't rise from the dead, all bishops, priests, and Christian ministers should go home and get honest jobs, and all the Christian faithful should leave their churches immediately.

As Paul himself put it: "If Christ has not been raised, then empty too is our preaching." It's no good, of course, trying to explain the Resurrection away or rationalize it as a myth, a symbol, or an inner subjective experience. None of that does justice to the novelty and sheer strangeness of the biblical message.

It comes down finally to this: if Jesus was not raised from death, Christianity is a fraud and a joke. But if he did rise from death, then Christianity is the fullness of God's revelation, and Jesus must be the absolute center of our lives. There is no third option.

Reflect: How can you share the Good News of the Resurrection of Jesus with others this Easter season?

APRIL 5, 2026

Easter Sunday of the Resurrection of the Lord

John 20:1–9 (or Matthew 28:1–10)

On the first day of the week, Mary of Magdala came to the tomb early in the morning, while it was still dark, and saw the stone removed from the tomb. So she ran and went to Simon Peter and to the other disciple whom Jesus loved, and told them, "They have taken the Lord from the tomb, and we don't know where they put him." So Peter and the other disciple went out and came to the tomb. They both ran, but the other disciple ran faster than Peter and arrived at the tomb first; he bent down and saw the burial cloths there, but did not go in. When Simon Peter arrived after him, he went into the tomb and saw the burial cloths there, and the cloth that had covered his head, not with the burial cloths but rolled up in a separate place. Then the other disciple also went in, the one who had arrived at the tomb first, and he saw and believed. For they did not yet understand the Scripture that he had to rise from the dead.

Friends, our Easter Gospel contains St. John's magnificent account of the Resurrection.

There are three key lessons that follow from the disquieting fact of the Resurrection. First, this world is not all there is. The Resurrection of Jesus from the dead shows as definitively as possible that God is up to something greater than we had imagined. We don't have to live as though death were our master and as though nihilism were the only coherent point of view. We can, in fact, begin to see this world as a place of gestation toward something higher, more permanent, more splendid.

Second, the tyrants know that their time is up. Remember that the cross was Rome's way of asserting its authority. But when Jesus was raised from the dead through the power of the Holy Spirit, the first Christians knew that Caesar's days were, in point of fact, numbered. The faculty lounge interpretation of the Resurrection as a subjective event or a mere symbol is exactly what the tyrants of the world want, for it poses no real threat to them.

Third, the path of salvation has been opened to everyone. Jesus went all the way down, journeying into pain, despair, alienation, even godforsakenness. He went as far as you can go away from the Father. Why? In order to reach all those who had wandered from God. In light of the Resurrection, the first Christians came to know that, even as we run as fast as we can away from the Father, we are running into the arms of the Son.

Let us not domesticate these still-stunning lessons of the Resurrection. Rather, let us allow them to unnerve us, change us, and set us on fire.

Reflect: Spend some time today reflecting on the shock of the empty tomb on Easter morning and one of these lessons that follow from it.

CONCLUSION

Friends,

In the name of the risen Lord, greetings! Lent is over and we've now moved into Easter. Alleluia!

I'd like to thank you for joining me on this journey through the Lenten season. Now that we've finished, you might be wondering, what's next? How do I maintain the spiritual momentum I developed during Lent? I'd like to suggest a few practical tips.

First, be sure to visit our website, wordonfire.org, on a regular basis. There you'll find lots of helpful resources, including new articles, videos, podcasts, and homilies, all designed to help strengthen your faith and evangelize the culture. The best part is that all of it is free!

In addition to those free resources, I invite you to join the Word on Fire Institute. This is an online hub of deep spiritual and intellectual formation, where you'll journey through courses taught by me and other fellows. Our goal is to build an army of evangelists, people who have been transformed by Christ and want to bring his light to the world. Learn more and sign up at wordonfire.institute.

Finally, consider carrying on your Lenten progress by grounding your life more concretely in the Eucharist, which is what keeps us alive spiritually. Are you only attending Mass on Sundays? Commit to attending one extra Mass each week. Is there a chapel nearby that offers Eucharistic Adoration? Sign up for a weekly hour of meditation and prayer before the Blessed Sacrament. The Eucharist is the alpha and the omega of Christian discipleship. It is the energy without which authentic Christianity runs down.

Again, thank you from all of us at Word on Fire, and God bless you during this Easter season!

Peace,

+ Robert Barron

Bishop Robert Barron

THE STATIONS OF

THE CROSS

Visit wordonfire.org/stations/ for
the Stations of the Cross with Bishop Barron.

All Stations of the Cross images are from the
Church of All Saints in Blato, Korcula Island, Croatia.

OPENING PRAYER

In the name of the Father, and of the Son,
and of the Holy Spirit.
Amen.

℣. Lord Jesus Christ, Son of God,
℟. Have mercy on me, a sinner.
℣. Lord Jesus Christ, Son of God,
℟. Have mercy on me, a sinner.
℣. Lord Jesus Christ, Son of God,
℟. Have mercy on me, a sinner.

The First Station

JESUS IS CONDEMNED TO DEATH

℣. We adore you, O Christ, and we bless you.
(Genuflect)
℟. Because by your holy cross you have redeemed the world.
(Rise)

Leader: Jesus stands before Pontius Pilate, the local representative of Caesar. Pilate, undoubtedly sure of his worldly power and authority, sizes up this criminal, asking, "Are you the King of the Jews?" Jesus responds, "My kingdom does not belong to this world. . . . For this I came into the world, to testify to the truth." Unimpressed, Pilate asks, "What is truth?" And then he condemns Jesus to death. *(Kneel)*

All pray: Lord Jesus, Israel dreamed of a new King who would defeat its enemies and reign over the whole world. You accomplished this through your cross and Resurrection, outmaneuvering the sin of the world and swallowing it up in the divine forgiveness. Help us to give our full allegiance to you each day, rejecting the old reign of violence and power and embracing your reign of nonviolence and love.

(Optional)

Our Father, who art in heaven,
hallowed be thy name;
thy kingdom come,
thy will be done
on earth as it is in heaven.
Give us this day our daily bread,
and forgive us our trespasses,
as we forgive those who trespass against us;
and lead us not into temptation,
but deliver us from evil.
Amen.

Hail Mary, full of grace, the Lord is with thee;
blessed art thou among women,
and blessed is the fruit of thy womb, Jesus.
Holy Mary, Mother of God,
pray for us sinners,
now and at the hour of our death.
Amen.

Glory be to the Father, and to the Son, and to the Holy Spirit; as it was in the beginning, is now, and ever shall be, world without end.
Amen.

(Rise)

All sing:

Stabat Mater dolorosa
Iuxta Crucem lacrimosa,
Dum pendebat Filius.

At the cross her station keeping,
Stood the mournful Mother weeping,
Close to Jesus to the last.

The Second Station

JESUS TAKES UP HIS CROSS

℣. We adore you, O Christ, and we bless you.
(Genuflect)
℟. Because by your holy cross you have redeemed the world.
(Rise)

Leader: God the Father sends his Son to the cross—not out of anger, but out of love; not to see him suffer, but to set things right. "For God so loved the world that he gave his only Son, so that everyone who believes in him might not perish but might have eternal life." God the Son willingly takes up that terrible cross—a sacrifice expressive of compassion for us sinners.
(Kneel)

All pray: Lord Jesus, you took up the cross; give us the grace to take up our cross daily and follow you. You lived in self-forgetting love unto death; give us the grace to be such love. You broke open your own heart for us; give us the grace to open our hearts for others.

(Optional)

Our Father, who art in heaven,
hallowed be thy name;
thy kingdom come,
thy will be done
on earth as it is in heaven.
Give us this day our daily bread,
and forgive us our trespasses,
as we forgive those who trespass against us;
and lead us not into temptation,
but deliver us from evil.
Amen.

Hail Mary, full of grace, the Lord is with thee;
blessed art thou among women,
and blessed is the fruit of thy womb, Jesus.
Holy Mary, Mother of God,
pray for us sinners,
now and at the hour of our death.
Amen.

Glory be to the Father, and to the Son, and to the Holy Spirit; as it was in the beginning, is now, and ever shall be, world without end.
Amen.

(Rise)

All sing:

Cuius animam gementem,
Contristatam et dolentem,
Pertransivit gladius.

Through her heart, his sorrow sharing,
All his bitter anguish bearing,
Now at length the sword had passed.

The Third Station

JESUS FALLS FOR THE FIRST TIME

℣. We adore you, O Christ, and we bless you.
(Genuflect)
℟. Because by your holy cross you have redeemed the world.
(Rise)

Leader: Jesus—crowned with thorns and already almost drained of blood—is made to carry his cross. As he makes his painful way to Calvary, bearing the burdens of the world's sin, he falls under the tremendous weight.
(Kneel)

All pray: Lord Jesus, we so often see the universe as turning around our egos and needs. Rescue us from the insanity of sin, which brings about spiritual disintegration and death. As you bore our burdens, disempowering them from within, may we actively lower ourselves to bear the burdens of others.

(Optional)

Our Father, who art in heaven,
hallowed be thy name;
thy kingdom come,
thy will be done
on earth as it is in heaven.
Give us this day our daily bread,
and forgive us our trespasses,
as we forgive those who trespass against us;
and lead us not into temptation,
but deliver us from evil.
Amen.

Hail Mary, full of grace, the Lord is with thee;
blessed art thou among women,
and blessed is the fruit of thy womb, Jesus.
Holy Mary, Mother of God,
pray for us sinners,
now and at the hour of our death.
Amen.

Glory be to the Father, and to the Son, and to the Holy Spirit; as it was in the beginning, is now, and ever shall be, world without end.
Amen.

(Rise)

All sing:

O quam tristis et afflicta
Fuit illa benedicta
Mater Unigeniti!

Oh, how sad and sore distressed
Was that Mother highly blest
Of the sole-begotten One!

The Fourth Station

JESUS MEETS HIS BLESSED MOTHER

℣. We adore you, O Christ, and we bless you.
(Genuflect)
℟. Because by your holy cross you have redeemed the world.
(Rise)

Leader: As he carries the cross, Jesus meets his Blessed Mother, the Virgin Mary. The humble handmaid through whom Christ was born now watches him approach his death, a sword of sorrow piercing her soul.
(Kneel)

All pray: Holy Mary, you followed your son all the way to the cross, where he entrusted us to you as our mother and the privileged channel of his grace. Intercede for us, that we might be drawn into deeper fellowship with him.

(Optional)

Our Father, who art in heaven,
hallowed be thy name;
thy kingdom come,
thy will be done
on earth as it is in heaven.
Give us this day our daily bread,
and forgive us our trespasses,
as we forgive those who trespass against us;
and lead us not into temptation,
but deliver us from evil.
Amen.

Hail Mary, full of grace, the Lord is with thee;
blessed art thou among women,
and blessed is the fruit of thy womb, Jesus.
Holy Mary, Mother of God,
pray for us sinners,
now and at the hour of our death.
Amen.

Glory be to the Father, and to the Son, and to the Holy Spirit; as it was in the beginning, is now, and ever shall be, world without end.
Amen.

(Rise)

All sing:

Quae moerebat, et dolebat,
Pia Mater, dum videbat
Nati poenas inclyti.

Christ above in torment hangs;
She beneath beholds the pangs
Of her dying glorious Son.

The Fifth Station

SIMON OF CYRENE IS MADE TO HELP JESUS BEAR THE CROSS

℣. We adore you, O Christ, and we bless you.
(Genuflect)
℟. Because by your holy cross you have redeemed the world.
(Rise)

Leader: The Romans, not wanting Christ to die before his Crucifixion, press into service Simon of Cyrene. How perilous and dangerous this must have seemed to Simon! But he seizes the moment and helps Jesus with the cross, bearing some of his suffering.
(Kneel)

All pray: Lord Jesus, at the moment of truth, Simon of Cyrene saw that you had need of him—and he responded. Help us, too, to see and respond to your need of us. Even if we are unnoticed or mocked, press us into service to bear you into the world.

(Optional)

Our Father, who art in heaven,
hallowed be thy name;
thy kingdom come,
thy will be done
on earth as it is in heaven.
Give us this day our daily bread,
and forgive us our trespasses,
as we forgive those who trespass against us;
and lead us not into temptation,
but deliver us from evil.
Amen.

Hail Mary, full of grace, the Lord is with thee;
blessed art thou among women,
and blessed is the fruit of thy womb, Jesus.
Holy Mary, Mother of God,
pray for us sinners,
now and at the hour of our death.
Amen.

Glory be to the Father, and to the Son, and to the Holy Spirit; as it was in the beginning, is now, and ever shall be, world without end.
Amen.

(Rise)

All sing:

Quis est homo qui non fleret,
Matrem Christi si videret
In tanto supplicio?

Is there one who would not weep,
Whelmed in miseries so deep
Christ's dear Mother to behold?

The Sixth Station

VERONICA WIPES THE FACE OF JESUS

℣. We adore you, O Christ, and we bless you.
(Genuflect)
℟. Because by your holy cross you have redeemed the world.
(Rise)

Leader: A woman called Veronica approaches and wipes the blood and sweat from Jesus' face as he continues his way to Calvary. An image of the face of Christ—the divine Word made flesh—is miraculously imprinted on her veil.
(Kneel)

All pray: Lord Jesus, in your Holy Face, we see the ugliness of our sin, which rules out our self-justification. But we also see the face of mercy, which lifts us from our self-reproach. In your agonies, you reveal our agony and take it away. Keep our gaze fixed on yours, and strengthen us in our mission of drawing the whole world toward you.

(Optional)

Our Father, who art in heaven,
hallowed be thy name;
thy kingdom come,
thy will be done
on earth as it is in heaven.
Give us this day our daily bread,
and forgive us our trespasses,
as we forgive those who trespass against us;
and lead us not into temptation,
but deliver us from evil.
Amen.

Hail Mary, full of grace, the Lord is with thee;
blessed art thou among women,
and blessed is the fruit of thy womb, Jesus.
Holy Mary, Mother of God,
pray for us sinners,
now and at the hour of our death.
Amen.

Glory be to the Father, and to the Son, and to the Holy Spirit; as it was in the beginning, is now, and ever shall be, world without end.
Amen.

(Rise)

All sing:

Quis non posset contristari
Christi Matrem contemplari
Dolentem cum Filio?

Can the human heart refrain
From partaking in her pain,
In that Mother's pain untold?

The Seventh Station

JESUS FALLS FOR THE SECOND TIME

℣. We adore you, O Christ, and we bless you.
(Genuflect)
℟. Because by your holy cross you have redeemed the world.
(Rise)

Leader: Under the overwhelming weight of the cross, Jesus falls a second time. Here is the suffering servant prophesied by Isaiah, who is wounded for our transgressions and crushed for our iniquities. By enduring the pain of the cross, he indeed bears our sins; by his stripes, we are indeed healed.
(Kneel)

All pray: Lord Jesus, you entered into our suffering and thereby sanctified it. Make us not only willing to suffer, but willing to suffer as you did, absorbing violence and hatred through our forgiveness and nonviolence.

(Optional)

Our Father, who art in heaven,
hallowed be thy name;
thy kingdom come,
thy will be done
on earth as it is in heaven.
Give us this day our daily bread,
and forgive us our trespasses,
as we forgive those who trespass against us;
and lead us not into temptation,
but deliver us from evil.
Amen.

Hail Mary, full of grace, the Lord is with thee;
blessed art thou among women,
and blessed is the fruit of thy womb, Jesus.
Holy Mary, Mother of God,
pray for us sinners,
now and at the hour of our death.
Amen.

Glory be to the Father, and to the Son, and to the Holy Spirit; as it was in the beginning, is now, and ever shall be, world without end.
Amen.

(Rise)

All sing:

Pro peccatis suae gentis
Vidit Iesum in tormentis,
Et flagellis subditum.

Bruised, derided, cursed, defiled,
She beheld her tender Child
All with bloody scourges rent.

The Eighth Station

JESUS MEETS THE WOMEN OF JERUSALEM

℣. We adore you, O Christ, and we bless you.
(Genuflect)
℟. Because by your holy cross you have redeemed the world.
(Rise)

Leader: As Jesus is led to Calvary, a great number follow him, including the weeping women of Jerusalem. Jesus turns to them and speaks as judge of the world, saying, "Daughters of Jerusalem, do not weep for me; weep instead for yourselves and for your children."
(Kneel)

All pray: Lord Jesus, you are the Savior who shows us the way out of our sin. But you are also the Judge who shows us we are sinners. Your every move, word, and gesture, especially your violent death, constituted God's judgment on the world. Whenever we are tempted to think that all is well with us, direct our gaze to your cross, where our illusions die.

(Optional)

Our Father, who art in heaven,
hallowed be thy name;
thy kingdom come,
thy will be done
on earth as it is in heaven.
Give us this day our daily bread,
and forgive us our trespasses,
as we forgive those who trespass against us;
and lead us not into temptation,
but deliver us from evil.
Amen.

Hail Mary, full of grace, the Lord is with thee;
blessed art thou among women,
and blessed is the fruit of thy womb, Jesus.
Holy Mary, Mother of God,
pray for us sinners,
now and at the hour of our death.
Amen.

Glory be to the Father, and to the Son, and to the Holy Spirit; as it was in the beginning, is now, and ever shall be, world without end.
Amen.

(Rise)

All sing:

Vidit suum dulcem Natum
Moriendo desolatum,
Dum emisit spiritum.

For the sins of his own nation,
Saw him hang in desolation,
Till his Spirit forth he sent.

The Ninth Station

JESUS FALLS FOR THE THIRD TIME

℣. We adore you, O Christ, and we bless you.
(Genuflect)
℟. Because by your holy cross you have redeemed the world.
(Rise)

Leader: Jesus continues to bear the terrible weight of the cross—a cross so heavy that it causes him to fall for a third time. Bearing the weight of our sin, and entering into our suffering, Jesus now rises to approach the final enemy to be defeated: death itself.
(Kneel)

All pray: Lord Jesus, at the root of sin is fear, especially fear of death. Thus, you journeyed into the realm of death and, by your sacrifice, twisted it back to life. You conquered death precisely by dying. Keep us from living in a world dominated by death and the fear of death, and help us to remember that death does not have the final word.

(Optional)

Our Father, who art in heaven,
hallowed be thy name;
thy kingdom come,
thy will be done
on earth as it is in heaven.
Give us this day our daily bread,
and forgive us our trespasses,
as we forgive those who trespass against us;
and lead us not into temptation,
but deliver us from evil.
Amen.

Hail Mary, full of grace, the Lord is with thee;
blessed art thou among women,
and blessed is the fruit of thy womb, Jesus.
Holy Mary, Mother of God,
pray for us sinners,
now and at the hour of our death.
Amen.

Glory be to the Father, and to the Son, and to the Holy Spirit; as it was in the beginning, is now, and ever shall be, world without end.
Amen.

(Rise)

All sing:

Eia Mater, fons amoris,
Me sentire vim doloris
Fac, ut tecum lugeam.

O thou Mother! fount of love!
Touch my spirit from above,
Make my heart with thine accord.

The Tenth Station

JESUS IS STRIPPED OF HIS GARMENTS

℣. We adore you, O Christ, and we bless you.
(Genuflect)
℟. Because by your holy cross you have redeemed the world.
(Rise)

Leader: The soldiers take Jesus' clothes and divide them into four shares, a share for each soldier, and cast lots for his tunic, fulfilling the words of the Psalm: "They divided my garments among them, and for my vesture they cast lots." Christ is stripped of everything: reputation, comfort, esteem, food, drink—even the pathetic clothes on his back.
(Kneel)

All pray: Lord Jesus, on the way of the cross, you despised the addictions of wealth, pleasure, power, and honor, and you loved the will of your Father. You were stripped naked, utterly detached from worldly goods. You went into the furthest reaches of godforsakenness in order to bring the divine love even to that darkest place. Grant that we may despise what you despised, and love what you loved.

(Optional)

Our Father, who art in heaven,
hallowed be thy name;
thy kingdom come,
thy will be done
on earth as it is in heaven.
Give us this day our daily bread,
and forgive us our trespasses,
as we forgive those who trespass against us;
and lead us not into temptation,
but deliver us from evil.
Amen.

Hail Mary, full of grace, the Lord is with thee;
blessed art thou among women,
and blessed is the fruit of thy womb, Jesus.
Holy Mary, Mother of God,
pray for us sinners,
now and at the hour of our death.
Amen.

Glory be to the Father, and to the Son, and to the Holy Spirit; as it was in the beginning, is now, and ever shall be, world without end.
Amen.

(Rise)

All sing:

Fac, ut ardeat cor meum
In amando Christum Deum
Ut sibi complaceam.

Make me feel as thou hast felt;
Make my soul to glow and melt
With the love of Christ my Lord.

The Eleventh Station

JESUS IS CRUCIFIED

℣. We adore you, O Christ, and we bless you.
(Genuflect)
℟. Because by your holy cross you have redeemed the world.
(Rise)

Leader: Jesus is crucified between two criminals, saying, "Father, forgive them, they know not what they do." Dying on a Roman instrument of torture, undergoing excruciating pain, he allows the full force of the world's hatred and dysfunction to wash over him, to spend itself on him. And he responds not with violence or resentment but with forgiveness.
(Kneel)

All pray: Lord Jesus, in your Crucifixion, you took away the sin of the world, swallowing it up in the divine mercy. Through your perfect sacrifice as high priest, eternal life has been made available to the whole of humanity. Stir up your Church to deepen its participation in this eternal act through the Mass, where we unite our sacrifices with yours.

(Optional)

Our Father, who art in heaven,
hallowed be thy name;
thy kingdom come,
thy will be done
on earth as it is in heaven.
Give us this day our daily bread,
and forgive us our trespasses,
as we forgive those who trespass against us;
and lead us not into temptation,
but deliver us from evil.
Amen.

Hail Mary, full of grace, the Lord is with thee;
blessed art thou among women,
and blessed is the fruit of thy womb, Jesus.
Holy Mary, Mother of God,
pray for us sinners,
now and at the hour of our death.
Amen.

Glory be to the Father, and to the Son, and to the Holy Spirit; as it was in the beginning, is now, and ever shall be, world without end.
Amen.

(Rise)

All sing:

Sancta Mater, istud agas,
Crucifixi fige plagas
Cordi meo valide.

Holy Mother! pierce me through;
In my heart each wound renew
Of my Savior crucified.

The Twelfth Station

JESUS DIES ON THE CROSS

℣. We adore you, O Christ, and we bless you.
(Genuflect)
℟. Because by your holy cross you have redeemed the world.
(Rise)

Leader: From the cross, Jesus says "Consummatum est"—"It is finished." The work of the Lord has been brought to fulfillment. He gives out a loud cry, and breathes his last. Above the crucified God hangs a sign placed by Pontius Pilate and written out in Hebrew, Greek, and Latin: "Jesus the Nazorean, the King of the Jews."
(Kneel)

All pray: Lord Jesus, you are the new David, the one who fulfills salvation history and finally rescues humanity. Help us to announce the message that Pilate first announced unwittingly, the message that every person was born to hear: that you are the new King.

(Optional)

Our Father, who art in heaven,
hallowed be thy name;
thy kingdom come,
thy will be done
on earth as it is in heaven.
Give us this day our daily bread,
and forgive us our trespasses,
as we forgive those who trespass against us;
and lead us not into temptation,
but deliver us from evil.
Amen.

Hail Mary, full of grace, the Lord is with thee;
blessed art thou among women,
and blessed is the fruit of thy womb, Jesus.
Holy Mary, Mother of God,
pray for us sinners,
now and at the hour of our death.
Amen.

Glory be to the Father, and to the Son, and to the Holy Spirit; as it was in the beginning, is now, and ever shall be, world without end.
Amen.

(Rise)

All sing:

Tui Nati vulnerati,
Tam dignati pro me pati,
Poenas mecum divide.

Let me share with thee his pain,
Who for all my sins was slain,
Who for me in torments died.

The Thirteenth Station

JESUS IS TAKEN DOWN FROM THE CROSS AND LAID IN THE ARMS OF MARY

℣. We adore you, O Christ, and we bless you.
(Genuflect)
℟. Because by your holy cross you have redeemed the world.
(Rise)

Leader: After the Crucifixion, Jesus is taken from the cross and laid in the arms of Mary, the definitive Ark of the Covenant, who carried the incarnate Word in her very womb. At his birth, Mary placed Jesus in a manger, where animals eat. Now, at his death, she presents him as food for the life of the world.
(Kneel)

All pray: Lord Jesus, the Blessed Virgin Mary cradled you in her arms. Marked with your blood, she presented your sacrifice to us and for us. In her offering of your body, may we be reminded of the Church's continual offering of your Body in the Eucharist.

(Optional)

Our Father, who art in heaven,
hallowed be thy name;
thy kingdom come,
thy will be done
on earth as it is in heaven.
Give us this day our daily bread,
and forgive us our trespasses,
as we forgive those who trespass against us;
and lead us not into temptation,
but deliver us from evil.
Amen.

Hail Mary, full of grace, the Lord is with thee;
blessed art thou among women,
and blessed is the fruit of thy womb, Jesus.
Holy Mary, Mother of God,
pray for us sinners,
now and at the hour of our death.
Amen.

Glory be to the Father, and to the Son, and to the Holy Spirit; as it was in the beginning, is now, and ever shall be, world without end.
Amen.

(Rise)

All sing:

Fac me tecum pie flere,
Crucifixo condolere,
Donec ego vixero.

Let me mingle tears with thee,
Mourning him who mourned for me,
All the days that I may live.

The Fourteenth Station

JESUS IS LAID IN THE TOMB

℣. We adore you, O Christ, and we bless you.
(Genuflect)
℟. Because by your holy cross you have redeemed the world.
(Rise)

Leader: Joseph of Arimathea, a secret admirer of Jesus, comes courageously to ask for the body of the Lord, and a group of women who had accompanied Jesus from Galilee watch carefully to see where he is buried. His enemies had closed in on him, and most of his intimate friends had fled in fear, but these faithful disciples stay with Jesus until the end.
(Kneel)

All pray: Lord Jesus, make our discipleship as complete and consistent as the women who followed you from Galilee to the grave. You went to the cross because you love your Father's will; let we who love you go to that same bitter end, knowing that the stone of our resting place will, like yours, be one day rolled away. Fill our hearts with the joy of the empty tomb, and make us bold in sharing the Good News of your Resurrection.

(Optional)

Our Father, who art in heaven,
hallowed be thy name;
thy kingdom come,
thy will be done
on earth as it is in heaven.
Give us this day our daily bread,
and forgive us our trespasses,
as we forgive those who trespass against us;
and lead us not into temptation,
but deliver us from evil.
Amen.

Hail Mary, full of grace, the Lord is with thee;
blessed art thou among women,
and blessed is the fruit of thy womb, Jesus.
Holy Mary, Mother of God,
pray for us sinners,
now and at the hour of our death.
Amen.

Glory be to the Father, and to the Son, and to the Holy Spirit; as it was in the beginning, is now, and ever shall be, world without end.
Amen.

(Rise)

All sing:

Iuxta Crucem tecum stare,
Et me tibi sociare
In planctu desidero.

By the cross with thee to stay;
There with thee to weep and pray;
Is all I ask of thee to give.

CLOSING PRAYER

From St. Thérèse of Lisieux's Act of Oblation to Merciful Love

All pray: I thank you, O my God, for all the graces you have granted me, especially the grace of making me pass through the crucible of suffering. It is with joy I shall contemplate you on the Last Day carrying the scepter of your cross. Since you deigned to give me a share in this very precious cross, I hope in heaven to resemble you and to see shining in my glorified body the sacred stigmata of your Passion.
Amen.

In the name of the Father, and of the Son,
and of the Holy Spirit.
Amen.

Do you wish you had a book with daily prayers and Scripture passages you could use beyond Lent?

The Liturgy of the Hours is the official prayer of the Church. It is an ancient, structured way of praying that focuses on the Psalms and helps us make Christ the center of every day.

Get started today at **wordonfire.org/pray.**